Juergen Glag

**Efficient Software Development
with DB2 for OS/390**

Efficient Software Development
Edited by Stephen Fedtke

This series of books covers special topics which are useful for programmers, team leaders, project managers, and businessmen involved in data processing.

The practical 'know-how' presented in this series comes from the authors' countless years of experience in programming and system development. Specifically, this series will help you to:
- reduce the costs of software application and development
- implement future-oriented strategies in data processing
- reduce training time and cost
- find efficient solutions for problems in all stages of the software life-cycle
- to ensure the rapid development of applications with the help of effective project management methods.

These books are practical guides from experts for experts. Those who read these books today will surely benefit from their knowledge tomorrow.

Books already in print:

Effizienter DB-Einsatz von ADABAS
von Dieter W. Storr

Effizienter Einsatz von PREDICT
Informationssysteme entwerfen und realisieren
von Volker Blödel

Effiziente NATURAL-Programmierung
von Sylvia Scheu

Handbuch der Anwendungsentwicklung
Wegweiser erfolgreicher Gestaltung von IV-Projekten
von Carl Steinweg

CICS und effiziente DB-Verarbeitung
Optimale Zugriffe auf DB2, DL/1 und VSAM-Daten
von Jürgen Schnell

QM-Optimizing der Softwareentwicklung
von Dieter Burgartz und Thomas Blum

Efficient Software Development with DB2 for OS/390
Organizational and Technical Measures for Performance Optimization
by Juergen Glag

Vieweg

Juergen Glag

Efficient Software Development with DB2 for OS/390

Organizational and Technical Measures
for Performance Optimization

Edited by Stephen Fedtke

Translated by Ursula Kollar-Friedrich

2nd, revised Edition

vieweg

Originally published in the German language by Friedr. Vieweg & Sohn Verlagsgesellschaft mbH,
D-65189 Wiesbaden, Germany under the titel 'Effiziente Softwareentwicklung mit DB2/MVS. Orga-
nisatorische und technische Maßnahmen zur Optimierung der Performance by Juergen Glag,
1. Auflage (1st Edition)'.
© Friedr. Vieweg & Sohn Verlagsgesellschaft mbH, Braunschweig/Wiesbaden, 1996,

1st Edition 1998
2nd Edition 1999

Vieweg is a subsidiary company of Bertelsmann Professional Information.

http://www.vieweg.de

Cover design: Ulrike Weigel, www.CorporateDesignGroup.de

Printed on acid-free paper

ISBN 978-3-528-15587-2

Preface

During the last few years, more and more data is stored in relational database systems which were stored in hierarchical database systems or in VSAM data sets before. In this respect, DB2 plays a leading role in big enterprises for the administration of business critical data. This new situation requires consideration of DB2 performance issues.

In many of these enterprises, the situation is indeed characterized by the fact that the staff is used to dealing with the pitfalls of VSAM or IMS due to many years of experience. Therefore, the resulting VSAM or IMS based applications are high-performance systems. The attempt, however, to apply on DB2 the same tuning measures as on the other systems is doomed to failure due to the different system structures. This is one of the reasons why DB2 has a reputation of preventing the generation of high performance systems.

Consequently, because of the singular system structure, other measures are necessary in order to realize high performance application systems.

This book is not a comprehensive basic work on DB2 but a manual for the solution of performance problems caused by the application systems' design. It is assumed that the system parameters are "right". The book shares a multitude of experiences gained through daily practice with numerous projects.

The first part systematically deals with the symptoms and the causes of and proven solutions for typical performance problems. With this knowledge, on the occurrence of problems the reader is able to locate their potential causes and to rapidly find solutions.

The second part contains case studies from daily practice. These examples were selected to be relevant to most users and immediately employable in the enterprise. The application of these examples will implement the required functionality in such a way that there is hardly any risk left for performance problems to occur.

The third part points out a tuning methodology for efficiently solving performance problems. In such a situation, on one hand it is important to rapidly achieve tangible results, on the other hand sufficient time will hardly be available to first develop an appropriate method and then to solve the problems. Such tuning can not be completely avoided - neither in a DB2 environment nor in other environments - but it can be minimized through the measures described in this book.

Next, there is a number of checklists and examples to be used again and again in daily practice.

Finally, compared to the first edition, the book is extended with a new chapter covering specially chosen topics in DDL and DML that help application development to build new applications more consistent and elegant. In doing so, error rate is usually reduced by an order of magnitude.

Jürgen Glag

September 1999

Table of Contents

1   Introduction 1

   1.1   Why this Book? 1

   1.2   Target Groups 3

2   Performance Problems: Symptoms, Causes, Measures 5

   2.1   Locking Problems 6
         2.1.1   Long Commit Intervals 6
         2.1.2   Executing Costly Operations 7
         2.1.3   Hot Spots 10

   2.2   Queuing Problems 14
         2.2.1   Similar Processing 14

   2.3   "Delivery Times Instead of Response Times" in On-line Operation 16
         2.3.1   Too Many IOs 16
         2.3.2   Physical Sorting of Large Result Sets 17
         2.3.3   Costly Queries 18
         2.3.4   Large Indexes 20
         2.3.5   Low Selectivity of Indexes 21

   2.4   Excessively Long Runtimes in Batch 23
         2.4.1   Extensive Business 23
         2.4.2   Too Many Synchronous IOs 23
         2.4.3   Processing Logic 24
         2.4.4   Too Many Indexes 26

   2.5   Summary 28

3   Organizational Measures in Software Development 30

   3.1   Application Scenario and Access Profile 31
         3.1.1   Application Scenario 32
         3.1.2   Access Profile 32

   3.2   Design of Critical Batch Runs 34
         3.2.1   Using Prefetch 35
         3.2.2   Load Procedure 39

   3.3   Access Modules 45

   3.4   Reducing Data Accesses 48

   3.5   Considerations Regarding the Application   Architecture 49

3.6   Standards for Software Development.................................... 50
    3.6.1   Programming Guidelines..................................... 50
    3.6.2   DB2 Manual 50

3.7   Using Quality Assurance Tools.. 52
    3.7.1   Static Quality Requirements 52
    3.7.2   Dynamic Quality Requirements......................... 54
    3.7.3   Usability Requirements on the QA Tool.............. 56

4   Case Studies **57**

4.1   Queues in On-line Operation.. 58
    4.1.1   Initial Situation.. 58
    4.1.2   Problem Description 60
    4.1.3   Approach... 60

4.2   Avoiding Hot-Spots.. 66
    4.2.1   Initial Situation.. 66
    4.2.2   Problem Description 68
    4.2.3   Approach... 69

4.3   Joins with Non-uniform Distribution of Attribute Values...................... 73
    4.3.1   Initial Situation.. 73
    4.3.2   Problem Description 75
    4.3.3   Approach... 75

4.4   Formulation of Restart Keys in Cursors 79
    4.4.1   Initial Situation.. 79
    4.4.2   Problem Description 80
    4.4.3   Approach... 81

4.5   Reducing Synchronous IOs for Hierarchical Structures...................... 82
    4.5.1   Initial Situation.. 82
    4.5.2   Problem Description 85
    4.5.3   Approach... 90

4.6   Comparison of LOAD and INSERT Procedures................ 92
    4.6.1   Initial Situation.. 92
    4.6.2   Problem Description 94
    4.6.3   Approach... 94

5   Tuning... **100**

5.1   Unavoidable Tuning Measures... 100

5.2   Economical Procedure with ABC Analysis........................ 101

5.3   Sequence of the Activities 102
    5.3.1   First Step: Providing Information....................... 102

	5.3.2	Second Step: Creating Access Profiles	102
	5.3.3	Third Step: Analysis of Access Profile and Explain	103
	5.3.4	Fourth Step: Analysis of the Tuning Candidates	103
5.4	Expenditure for Tuning		108
5.5	Effort Minimization for Future Tuning Measures		108
5.6	Adjustment of the Procedure Model		109
5.7	Staff Training		109
5.8	Measuring the Tuning Results/Success		110
6	**Checklists**		**111**
6.1	Checklist for the Application Development		111
	6.1.1	Tasks of the Application Developers	111
	6.1.2	Avoidance of Costly Instructions	112
	6.1.3	Using Literature	112
	6.1.4	Knowledge of Programmers	112
	6.1.5	Further Problem Causes	112
6.2	Tasks of a DBA Group		113
	6.2.1	Service for Application Development	113
	6.2.2	Defining Standards and Conventions	113
	6.2.3	Monitoring the Production Systems	113
	6.2.4	Quality Assurance	113
6.3	Application Scenario		114
6.4	Access Profile		115
6.5	Checklist for System Design		117
	6.5.1	Application System	117
	6.5.2	Program Design	117
	6.5.3	Job Design	118
	6.5.4	Database Design	118
6.6	Evaluating the DB2 Catalog for Critical Objects		119
	6.6.1	Critical Tables	119
	6.6.2	Critical Table Spaces	122
	6.6.3	Critical Indexes	122
	6.6.4	Critical Packages	124
6.7	Inverting a Timestamp		125
7	**Some Additional Stuff for Application Development**		**127**
7.1	DML Extensions		127
	7.1.1	AS-Clause	127

7.1.2		CASE-Expression	130
7.1.3		JOIN-Types	133
7.1.4		SYSDUMMY1-Table	137
7.2	DDL Extensions		138
7.2.1		WITH RESTRICT ON DROP clause	138
7.2.2		Type 2 Indexes	139
7.2.3		Row Level Locking	140
7.2.4		UR – Uncommitted Read	141
7.2.5		Stored Procedures	143

Bibliography 147

Index 148

1 Introduction

1.1 Why this Book?

Passing
experience

This book passes the experiences gained from working in a number of large scale productive DB2 environments. Indeed, it turns out that most performance problems occur either from a specific critical transaction load onwards or in connection with especially large tables.

Creation of
favorable basic
conditions

The application of "optimal" SQL alone will not suffice to provide lasting solutions to performance problems. What is more, a number of basic conditions must "be right" before one has the necessary security in software development enabling the development of high performance systems. The following chapters in this book will detail a number of measures which provide for developing better systems. By the way, it is the management of an enterprise that is responsible for the existence of these basic conditions, not the individual software developer.

Disproving
prejudices
concerning DB2
performance

The reader will not only obtain recommendations for activities to create appropriate basic conditions. There is also an intensive discussion of symptoms, causes, and measures of performance problems as well as a number of case studies. These will provide arguments for revealing the reproach to be heard again and again from many enterprises as a mere prejudice that it is impossible to develop high performance systems in large-scale productive environments with DB2.

These reproaches, or prejudices, are mostly heard from companies that operate extensive IMS environments for decades and therefore have IMS experience lasting for decades while the experiences with DB2 are not equally well-founded. A related prejudice says that DB2 is at best suited for the operation of inquiry systems such as, for example, Warehouse systems. In most cases, the cause of these prejudices are attributable to the ignorance of DB2 specifics.

Measures for
economical
software
development

From many years of dealing with DB2, specific and often organizational measures emanate that allow -- to a large extent --
for the prevention of the most frequent performance problems.
In operational practice this is significant inasmuch as performance problems cause basically unforeseen costs. The following
chapters will explain the measures to be taken in more detail.

Performance is
more than optimal
SQL

As mentioned above, using "optimal" SQL does not guarantee
high performance systems but is at best a necessary prerequisite. In this connection, SQL is to be understood as the so-
called DML, Data Manipulation Language, with instructions
such as INSERT, UPDATE, DELETE, and SELECT. Precisely
this language set is normally used in application programs. If
these instructions are optimally coded or subsequently optimized in the course of tuning measures, the impact of these
measures relating to an entire application system is always local, i.e., limited to the modified program. Obviously, this measure is only relatively slightly effective for performance improvements for extensive software systems. The following chapters
will describe measures with more global effects. Therefore, this
book assumes knowledge of SQL.

1.2   Target Groups

The essential target groups with their subjects of interest can be derived from the aim of this book to point out the organizational and technical measures that ensure efficient application systems.

DP management

This book supports the DP management in creating appropriate basic conditions for the development of high performance software systems.

Persons
responsible for
methods, tools,
and quality
assurance

The persons responsible for methods, tools, and quality assurance have to secure that newly developed application systems run with high performance. To do so, they mostly employ a procedure model and quality checks. The exhaustive treatment of organizational measures, standards, and supporting tools within this book will facilitate their tasks.

Project managers
and project leaders

Project managers or project leaders are essentially responsible for the compliance with the project objectives and for the coordination of the tasks. The basic, purely formal, project objectives consist of keeping to planned costs and schedules. A project manager or leader will fulfill his or her tasks better the more he or she can reduce risks early. One of the risks for compliance with the objectives is unforeseen and usually not budgeted. This risk is the refinishing of operations that become necessary due to the bad efficiency of the generated application system. Therefore, it is in his or her own interest that the measures ensuring performance are taken. Such measures consist, for example, in creating specific project and documentation results and in planning cost and date related quality assurance measures as early as in the first project planning phase. Chapter 5 is devoted to hints on the organization and planning of tuning projects in a narrower sense. It describes the course of several tuning projects performed in the past and the experiences gained by them.

Software
developers

For software developers, two aspects of this book are of special interest. On the one hand, it is important to see the reasons for imposed rules and standards. Otherwise, these are felt to be "pieces of malice" of a Methods and Tools department who in some developers' eyes knows nothing about software development anyway. If, however, a developer realizes that he or she generates improved systems when complying with specific standards, he or she will hardly balk at these measures. On the other hand, this book can also support him/her to locate performance problems faster and, therefore, to repair them faster.

Data base administrators

After introducing a new software system in production, a data base administrator (DBA) is often the one who makes the system actually operate. Within the shortest time, the DBA must carry out the tuning measures which were not considered during the development phase. In such a situation, he or she can hardly keep up with his/her real tasks such as, for example, production monitoring. The DBA's interest essentially is to force specific measures in software development in order to enable the generation of high performance systems right from the start. He or she should push, for example, that a system can be introduced in production only if specific results were generated during the development process and/or if he/she was consulted or notified in specific project phases. This means sooner or later that specific measures are adopted as standards.

For the system programming staff, persons responsible for the data center operation, and for further DBA tasks, other literature is of greater importance such as, for example, the Installation Guide, Administration Guide, and other manuals for system software closely related to DB2.

2 Performance Problems: Symptoms, Causes, Measures

A bunch of measures
in case of performance problems

In this chapter, we will explain the various causes starting with the typical symptoms that appear in application systems when there are performance problems. This explanation is followed by concrete hints as to which remedial measures can be taken to combat these problems. That favorite saying of American specialists holds true here: "It depends". This should be understood to mean that these measures are not a cure-all, but have solved a problem in *specific* situations in a *specific* technical environment. Furthermore, remember that normally there is not just *one* cause for a problem, but several. The same applies to the solution of the problem. Depending on the existing technical environment, there are almost always several possible approaches.

Let's start with the symptoms which the viewer notices when there are performance problems:

- locking problems,
- queuing problems,
- "delivery times instead of response times" in on-line operation,
- runtimes too long for batch processing.

There are many causes for each of these symptoms. A systematic discussion of the causes follows below, arranged according to the symptoms.

2.1   Locking Problems

Causes of
locking problems

There are a number of causes for locking problems. This cate-gory of problems is not caused only by excessively long commit intervals, but also because of intensive operations on table spaces and indexes.

The following causes come into consideration for locking prob-lems:

- long commit intervals (operations),

- execution of costly operations,

- hot spots.

2.1.1   Long Commit Intervals

Avoiding locking
for long periods

When a cause, usually a batch program, locks a resource -- be it a table space page or an index page -- for a very long time because it is not frequently issuing COMMIT commands or not at all, concurrent access to these locked resources is hindered. In this, it is completely immaterial whether the competing pro-gram is a batch program or an on-line transaction.

In on-line operations, it rarely happens that a transaction holds resources for an excessively long time. This is because in CICS, a SYNCPOINT is automatically set, at the latest, on sending the screen; this initiates a COMMIT in DB2. On the other hand, manually programmed SYNCPOINTs for shortening the locking periods usually don't make sense from the applica-tions' point of view.

COMMIT in
batches

Hence, issuing of COMMIT commands is essentially restricted to batch operations. Except for extremely short batches that run within a few minutes, it is absolutely necessary for all batch programs that they should issue COMMIT commands at regular intervals. This simultaneously provides another desired effect: in case of aborts, the entire run need not be repeated, instead it can be resumed at the last COMMIT point. However, this re-quires that restart logic is included in every batch program. In-cidentally, this is a rewarding field of activity with high value for the "Methods and Tools" department that exists in almost all companies.

Checkpoint table

The method of setting up a generalized table for checkpoint in-formation that is valid system-wide has proved successful. Job name, step name, and start time of execution come into consideration as key columns; the checkpoint-area is a character field of sufficient length. The contents of this field is program-specific since the data to be stored have different formats everywhere, e.g., access keys and working-storage fields of the program.

On program start, depending on whether it is a new start or a restart, either a first record is written to the checkpoint table, or the last suitable record from the aborted processing is read. This provides the information from what access key onwards processing is to be continued. For data integrity, it is important that when writing the changes the checkpoint table information should be written immediately before the COMMIT command.

Regarding the checkpoint frequency, in a number of companies a combined method of writing activity-controlled and time-controlled checkpoints proved to be an acceptable solution.

Locking problems resulting from intensive operations on table spaces or indexes usually occur because of the following causes.

2.1.2   Executing Costly Operations

Intensification of the problem in the case of many indexes

The term "costly operations" particularly refers to the SQL commands INSERT and DELETE. If these commands are executed frequently in programs, there may be locking conflicts with other requesters. Locking conflicts are almost certain since these commands do not only lock the table space page, or even several pages in case of bulk deletions, but to some extent, large index ranges as well. The problem is aggravated for table spaces if the records have a short length since the usually appropriate lock at page level applies to several rows. With multiple indexes to the addressed tables, the INSERT or DELETE activity is increased drastically. There is even the danger of deadlocks when several requesters are active with write access via various access paths.

Several methods proved successful for this problem cause under specific basic conditions.

Replacing DELETE statements by UPDATE statements

The method with the least side effects, hence acting almost exclusively local, is to replace the DELETE statement by an UPDATE statement on an extra field. This field indicates the logical validity of the record. For this purpose, the table must be extended by exactly that field. Depending on the requirements of the application, this would be a character field for a code, a DATE or a TIMESTAMP field. In the case of DATE or TIMESTAMP formats, the option WITH DEFAULT must not be set for CREATE TABLE. As far as possible, this extra validity field should not be included in an index since it might have the reverse effect on optimization due to a large number of index updates. All read operations on the table then refer to this field as well, in addition to the existing previous conditions. In INSERT operations, it is filled with either the smallest or the greatest permissible value. For the DATE format, the values are 0001-01-01 or 9999-12-31 respectively. For the TIMESTAMP format the values are 0001-01-01-00.00.00.000000 or 9999-12-31.24.00.00.000000 respectively. If the option WITH DEFAULT were set and if no value were given for the INSERT, the current timestamp would be taken, which would flag the record as invalid.

Increasing PCTFREE

It is also possible to ease the locking problem when executing costly commands by specifying a high free space parameter, i.e., PCTFREE value. Note that this parameter is only relevant for the LOAD and REORG utilities. An initially empty table to which only insertions are made does not have any free space, even if defined in the table definition. Assuming a good reorganization level of the table, i.e., the free space definition is effective, a high PCTFREE specification ensures that there is less information on one page. At this point, it should be mentioned that in such situations, the reorganization level and the free space of the index or the indexes has greater significance than that of the table spaces. If the table grows with time, the relation between INSERT and the existing rows drops. In this situation, it may be checked to what extent the free space parameters for table space and indexes can be lowered. The simplest method to do so is via ALTER INDEX ... PCTFREE ... or ALTER TABLESPACE ... PCTFREE ... and a subsequent REORG of the object.

Partitioned table spaces

In the case of large partitioned table spaces, this specification can be set at partition level. This is often a good idea if the clustering index has a time component. In such a scenario, hardly any INSERT operations, or none at all, are performed on the old partitions. Instead, many SELECT operations are. On the new partitions, the access profile is exactly the opposite, i.e., a high relative proportion of INSERT operations. For such a table, it is appropriate to set a low PCTFREE percentage, even zero, for the old partitions with few changes and a high

PCTFREE percentage for the new ones. On these partitions, the REORG utilities should then be run at a sufficiently high frequency so that the pre-settings become and remain effective.

Using loading procedures

Unfortunately, the INSERT statement cannot be as easily replaced by another SQL command as the DELETE statement. For this statement, you will have to check whether a load procedure is an appropriate alternative.

Read only, Warehouse data

For the simplest case in which, for instance, a Warehouse table is regenerated in weekly or monthly intervals and with no INSERT commands on this table, a load utility is almost always more economical. This includes both the time required for the generation as well as the achievable reorganization degree of the table.

If, in one run, more than 10 percent of the rows are inserted in a table, you should check whether unloading the table, followed by SORT, LOAD REPLACE LOG NO, and FULLCOPY might be more favorable. Whereas the INSERT commands considerably burden the log data sets when bulk inserts are made, this does not happen with the alternative LOAD utility. Incidentally, after bulk inserts, it is imperative, for security reasons, to run a FULLCOPY so that the times required for the RECOVER utilities do not become unreasonable. Thus, the time required for the bulk INSERTs plus FULLCOPY should be weighed against the total time spent for the UNLOAD, SORT, and LOAD steps.

Reducing indexes

Another proven method for eliminating or at least easing the locking problems for costly commands is to reduce the indexes on the concerned tables. Precisely, the INSERT and DELETE commands burden the indexes. If there are several indexes on a table -- the critical limit for operational tables would be about 3 indexes -- the risk of synchronous IOs increases disproportionately. Owing to the fact that the required index pages are practically never all present in the buffer pool, they must first be synchronously fetched from disk. Rewriting of these pages takes place asynchronously as well so that it cannot be attributed to the causing request. However, this method is somewhat problematical in that it does not just affect the current program with its costly commands, but all accesses to that table in other programs, too. Only after checking all accesses is it possible to decide whether the number of indexes can be reduced. Some indexes may have been created only as a precaution, and can hence be omitted. Sometimes the total number of indexes can also be reduced by redefining indexes. For instance, if there are two multi-column indexes with common first columns and different columns thereafter, they can be combined to form one index with all the fields of both the indexes. This method may discriminate the accesses that hitherto took place using the index that has been omitted, but the modification operations on this table are considerably favored.

2.1.3   Hot Spots

Another cause of locking problems is hot spots. Hot spots often result from an ascending key being defined for a table. The key can be a serial number or a timestamp. If all the requesters active at a particular time operate on the same page, the locking conflict is pre-programmed.

Problems with keys in ascending order

For locking problems resulting from hot spots, there is no local solution that is limited to one SQL statement and achievable by changing this statement. Hot spots are a problem at table level and can be solved only at that level.

Here is an example. Table T1 is given, with a serial number as clustering index.

```
CREATE TABLE T1
          (serno
          ,attribute-1
          ,attribute-2
          ,...
          ,attribute-n)
...
CREATE INDEX I1 ON T1
          (serno)
UNIQUE
CLUSTER
...
```

If several rows are to be simultaneously inserted into this table with the ascending key serno, then that is always done according to the index definition on the last page of the table.

| PAGE 1 | PAGE 2 | PAGE 3 | . . . | last PAGE |

Thus, everything is happening only on the last page of the table. That page is becoming a hot spot.

A hot spot is characterized by several requesters wanting to work simultaneously on one page. Hot spots can occur at both the table level as well as at the index level, being more difficult to recognize at the index level. As a further differentiation, a table without an index or with a time based index that is accessed by only one requester at a time does not have a hot spot, i.e., a task. The only common thing is that the index has a time reference.

Distributed keys

How can this problem be solved? Hot spots can be avoided by suitably distributing the keys. To do this, two components are required: an encoding and a decoding routine. Using such a construction, the application can continue to work with the original key since it need not know the actual key being stored in the table. The central routine that is called before and after the SQL commands takes care of encoding and decoding.

Inverting keys

A relatively simple method -- which also entails little overhead -- is the inversion of the key. This means reading the key from the right to the left. In the example mentioned above, the rows would not be inserted with the key values 12345, 12346, 12347, 12348, and 12349 during a given time interval, but with the values read from the right to the left: 54321, 64321, 74321, 84321, and 94321. You will notice immediately that the key values are distributed differently compared to the original situation. Moreover, this method is quite straight-forward since the key and the inverted key can be derived directly from each other without any further information being required.

For keys consisting of a serial number, the method presents no difficulty because both the original key as well as the inverted key have the same format. Thus, the same data format can be used for the inverted key and for the original key.

Inverting timestamps

If the time-based key is a timestamp, optimization presents itself. Since the memory requirements of the internal and external representation of the timestamp are drastically different -- 10 bytes as compared to 26 bytes -- and the inverted key no longer has the TIMESTAMP format, the index would be considerably bigger. Possibly even the index level would increase. Here, the special characters hyphen and dot should be removed on conversion in order to achieve a numeric result with 20 digits remaining. These digits should be inverted, i.e., the last digit at the beginning, the second-last on the second position, etc., and filled in hexadecimal format to a character field of 10 bytes length. This procedure is somewhat *tricky*, but even works in COBOL with several intermediate fields. This procedure allows you to maintain the index length completely unchanged. The hot spot could thus be removed without any negative side effects on the index level. For an example listing, refer to section 6.7.

The solution becomes more difficult if the table is being built up with a time-based key without using initial contents. In such a situation, key inversion alone does not suffice. In fact, it can be harmful because the distributed processing without free space being available can relatively quickly cause page-splits at the index level. The effects at runtime would then be similar to a comparable situation with a VSAM file.

Loading initial contents

In this situation, the following method proved helpful: in the initial stage, initial contents should be loaded in such a table. A very high PCTFREE value, both at table space level as well as at index level, is previously specified for the table. The index-related entry is more important. This specification can be set either when creating the table using the CREATE TABLE command or when subsequently changing the table using an ALTER command. The PCTFREE setting actually becomes effective only through executing the LOAD or REORG utility. In contrast, an INSERT command does not take into account the PCTFREE specification. Depending on the available disk space, a value of 80% or higher should be set. At the same time, you should think of marking the rows with the initial contents in any field in order to be able to recognize these rows later and to remove them simply with an SQL statement. This method is known by the term "preload". With the pages being previously set up, both at table level as well as at index level, the risk of page splits is considerably reduced. Now, the distributing of the key through inversion is given a turn again since the insertions are made into the previously built up pages in a distributed manner, i.e., without hot spots.

Frequent reorganization

During the first processing of this table, it may be necessary to run a REORG very frequently, perhaps even daily. Here too, the reorganization of the index is of greater importance, since an index page normally contains significantly more entries than a table space page. Locks on an index page thus affect considerably more rows than a lock on a table space page, and lead to greater hindrances.

2.2   Queuing Problems

By queuing problems, the formation of queues owing accesses to the DB2 tables is meant. Thus, this problem category is closely related to the locking problems, since no queue would form if the resources were free.

Nonetheless, queues differ from locking problems by their causes.

The most important causes for queuing problems are:

- similar processing,
- hot spots.

2.2.1   Similar Processing

Same processing sequence

It may well sound paradoxical, but one of the causes of queues is good programming style. If in one processing unit several tables are to be accessed for modification, high load will result in either queues or deadlocks. Good programming style is characterized by resources always being accessed in the same sequence, i.e., first always `Table1`, then `Table2`, and finally `Table3`. If a requester accesses a different sequence, there is the risk that the resource being currently required is locked by another requester, who in turn wishes to access a resource which the first requester has already locked. This is the classic deadlock situation.

Queuing problems due to the processing sequence always being similar can be solved by procedures like those being used in the case of locking problems.

Queuing occurs frequently if the entry table of a processing is time-based.

An example from the insurance industry: In a policy management system, particularly when creating new policies, there are several participating tables. Simplified, these are the policy table (*basic data*), the risk table (*what is insured?*), and the hazards table (*against what is the risk covered?*). There are 1:n relationships between the tables. Now, if the policy number is assigned in sequence, all requesters that create new records work on the very same page. They would be sequenced through the policy table until their respective predecessor has set its `COMMIT` point and releases its lock on the policy table.

Since the creation of such a new record involves extensive data entry and verification, there can be massive queuing problems.

Distributing keys

Such problems can be avoided by distributing the policy numbers -- similar to the procedure described in the section on locking. This procedure makes use of an internal key, which is used for the clustering index. The access to the table is managed by another external key. Of course, an index will generally also be required for this key. The problem of queuing due to a hot spot is thus transformed into the other potential problem that may result from setting up another index in conjunction with a high insert ratio.

This example illustrates the main problem of application tuning. There are few solutions to problems without side-effects. This is also evidence for the validity of the American saying on solutions to problems "It depends" -- it always depends on the basic conditions.

Blocking the
SQL commands

Another method for shortening the locking times in a processing unit involves a special programming technique. Instead of executing the SQL statements distributed between two COMMIT points, they should, as far as possible, be executed in succession without too much code between them. Let us assume an interval between two COMMIT points of one minute. Now, if a lock is set with, for example, an INSERT statement at the beginning of this interval, it is kept for almost one minute. If, however, all SQL statements are placed and executed at the end of the processing unit, the locks are active for a very short time. By using this programming technique, considerably more competing accesses can generally be performed without hindrance.

The next cause of queuing problems is bad DB design, namely, a hot spot.

For approaches to the hot spot problem refer to the section on locking problems (section 2.1).

2.3 "Delivery Times Instead of Response Times" in On-line Operation

For this category of problems, too, there are many causes that can be divided into several classes. The most important causes are:

- too many IOs,
- physical sorting of large result sets,
- complex queries,
- large indexes,
- low selectivity of indexes.

2.3.1 Too Many IOs

The first cause to be mentioned is an excessively high number of IOs. This cause will be described in further detail.

Many synchronous IOs

Firstly, "delivery times" may be caused by performing too many synchronous IOs. This means that every read or write access on a record requires one access to the hard disk. This implies, on the one hand, that for this type of processing the DB2 buffer pool is not used -- using the buffer pool normally drastically accelerates processing. On the other hand, it is implied that the provision of data is not a fast main memory operation, but a relatively slower disk access. This problem is often caused by the fact that important and frequent accesses are not supported by the clustering index -- emphasis being on the term clustering. For this index, the rows in the data pages are organized in sorted order -- provided that the reorganization state of the table spaces is good. In the case of a cursor processing, for example, which is supported by the clustering index, only very few data pages may have to be read for fetching several rows, instead of one data page for every row. By a suitable definition of this index and by using it properly, it is often possible to accelerate accesses by a factor of 10 and more.

Incorporating all conditions in the SQL statement

But too many IOs may also be a result of queries searching through too many data pages. Often, this is due to the fact that the query formulation does not include all restrictive conditions; instead, further filtering is done in the application program after every FETCH of a cursor. This programming technique is particularly popular among experienced programmers from the IMS

DB environment who are working with DB2 for the first time. As a result of this technique, the database cannot perform IO reduction, but must provide an excessively and needlessly large result set to the application program.

The approaches for this problem are almost obvious: in order to minimize the DB2 activities when providing application data, all the conditions that can be specified in a WHERE clause should be specified.

Dispensing with
programmed joins

In addition, too many IOs are caused by programmed joins. Here too, the rule applies that it is usually preferable to formulate joins in the SQL statement, since less data has to be transported thanks to improved index utilization. It is important that the join criterion on the inner table, i.e., the table that is addressed later, be supported by an index. Otherwise a scan, i.e., a sequential search, will be initiated on the table.

Caution with
referential integrity

Using RI (referential integrity) can be another cause for too many IOs. In the case of bulk insert operations on the lower level table, e.g., when inserting many order items to an order, on the INSERT of each item it is checked as to whether the upper level order exists. This can result in considerable overhead. The like also applies to DELETE operations with option CASCADE on the upper level table. Here, the DELETE operations on the lower level table are executed in a relatively costly way. To make matters worse, it is difficult to assign this process to the causing task, even using technical system related means. Hence, the use of RI must be considered very carefully from performance point of view.

2.3.2   Physical Sorting of Large Result Sets

Reducing the re-
sult sets

Another cause of "delivery times" is cursor processing with large result sets in conjunction with physical sorting. Cursor processing of large result sets without physical sorting is not as critical, nor sorting of small result sets of cursors. It is the combination of both circumstances that causes problems. It should go without saying that a cursor should always be formulated with an ORDER BY clause, so that the provision of the result is independent of the table's reorganization state.

Possible approaches in this context are to reduce the result sets on the one hand and to support sorting through suitable indexes on the other hand.

By reducing the result sets -- which can often be achieved by including additional clauses in the WHERE condition -- the response time of the queries can be improved considerably. Often, as already mentioned above, not all the conditions are included in the SQL statement, but instead are checked later in the program. With such a programming style, too much data is transferred to the program. Even for the data being superfluous later on, the entire process of data provision by the components Buffer Manager, Data Manager, and Relational Data System have to be executed, with the Relational Data System component being of particular importance.

Carefully selecting clustering index

By suitably defining the indexes, especially by carefully selecting the clustering index, physical sorting of large result sets can be avoided. The difficulty arises to harmonize this objective with the conflicting objective of setting up as few indexes as possible on tables.

2.3.3   Costly Queries

Costly queries can cause excessively long response times in multiple respects.

Unfavorable access path in case of join

The first possible reason may be that the Optimizer selected an unfavorable access path for a join. "Unfavorable" here means that the reduction of the result sets on the tables takes place late in their processing sequence. In the case of a query which performs a join on three tables and, because of the WHERE condition, qualifies 10,000 rows on the first, 1,000 rows on the second, and 10 rows on the third table, the reduction of the rows resulting from the cursor takes place only very late. Hence, this query will be rather costly, even if the join conditions are supported by indexes, since it causes many pages to be moved. If the access path could be influenced to process Table3 first, the query could provide the data much faster.

Checking catalog values

In this situation, you need to check whether the correct column information was available at BIND time when the access path was defined. Therefore, first check whether the RUNSTATS utility has run on the corresponding tables. This error, which is actually trivial, occurs astonishingly frequently.

Other influences on the access path can be anything from tricky to problematical. Catalog manipulation and query manipulation do provide some solutions. Both methods must be well documented, so that they do not drop the next time the table or the

query is changed. In particular, query manipulations with redundant clauses that do not make any changes to the result set
should be critically observed when releases or versions are
changed. This is important because they are based on specific
properties of a particular release level. In case of improvements to the Optimizer, these manipulations could result in
considerable runtime risks.

Restricting number
of tables in case of
joins

The second possible reason for costly queries is too many tables being addressed in one join. In this case, however, a
query optimization is futile. Multi-path joins, i.e., joins address-
ing more than four tables, are caused by the database design
or, rather, by the missing database design. According to experience, in such a case the conceptual data model is implemented in the database without any changes. This procedure
may be acceptable for small amounts of data, or for systems
that are not used much. However, in case of applications with
large amounts of data or excessive load in on-line operation,
problems will inevitably occur. The measures for optimizing a
multi-path join will be costly because the number of participating
tables can only be reduced by revising the table design.

Since the approaches suited for this cause interfere with the table design, they are always associated with additional effort and
cost.

Introducing
redundant fields

The first option is fairly well known: redundant fields are included in some tables to reduce the number of tables being addressed. What is costly in this solution is secure administration
of the redundant fields. On the one hand, more programming
and testing efforts are incurred. On the other hand, the additional maintenance of the redundant fields causes overhead for
the running system.

Pre-loading tables

Under certain basic conditions, there is another solution to the
problem, known as "pre-loading". If the participating tables are
modified rotationally only, the problematical join can set up an
additional table. This happens across the extent of all the tables. Hence, the join is not qualified with only one key as it
would normally be done. But instead, the tables are merely
joined with the existing join criteria. The result set from this join
is then used as input to load the new table. On this table, in
turn, an index is defined, which consists of the above mentioned access key for the single call. Thus, the multi-path join
has become a simple table access which is far less costly in
terms of runtime. What is costly in this solution is the imple-

mentation of the automatic loading process subsequent to the rotational modification of the initial tables. It appears to be important here that the process should run fully automatically in order to eliminate manual sources of errors.

Avoiding sub-queries

A third cause may be that instead of a join, a relatively complicated sub-query was formulated. In most cases, sub-queries can -- and should! -- be replaced by a suitable join. Exceptions to this are, for example, sub-queries with NOT EXISTS clauses. As a rule, the formulation as a join would be considerably less costly.

2.3.4 Large Indexes

Large tables are encountered mainly in large-scale production environments -- a fact that is also important from a performance point of view. This situation is also rather reassuring, since large quantities of data often indicate that the company you are working for has plenty of business.

Reducing index level

Nonetheless, it must be stated here as well that indexes are often not defined with sufficient care. In the case of large tables, there is the latent danger that index level 4 or even 5 is reached. This information can be easily read from the DB2 catalog, ideally after a RUNSTATS.

```
SELECT
        C.NAME
       ,C.NLEVELS
FROM
        SYSIBM.SYSINDEXES C
WHERE
        C.NLEVELS > 3
```

The jump to these index levels usually results in a significant deterioration of access times to the concerned table. This is easily explained. Owing to the large number of index pages, especially leaf-pages, these very pages will not normally all be located in the buffer pool, but must be synchronously fetched from disk. Thus, beyond the synchronous accesses to the data pages, which cannot generally be avoided for single SELECTs, there are additional synchronous accesses to index pages. As a result, an access to the concerned table is significantly costlier than to a table with index level 3 or less.

Reducing the number of index columns

What does index level 4 or higher originate from? Mostly, the index is defined in order to avoid sorting when accessing the cursor. Thus, all the fields of the WHERE and the ORDER BY condition are included in the index. Consequently, the index will then consist of possibly many fields. A pragmatic limit should be set at five fields. In most cases, it is sufficient to include the fields of the WHERE condition in the index definition. A positive effect on the index size can thus be achieved.

Sometimes, several almost redundant indexes, each with several fields, are defined on one table. This is done for the reasons already mentioned: to support all cursor accesses through indexes in such a way that no sorting need be done, as can be seen from the EXPLAIN. It is a good idea to avoid sorting, especially for large result sets. However, it is necessary to balance between a number of indexes as small as possible and an index level as low as possible. Hence, two competing objectives, each valid by itself, have to be reconciled.

Combining redundant indexes

One approach for this problem whose effects need to be investigated, is the combination of almost redundant indexes to reduce the total number of indexes to a table. Care must be taken here, that lengthening the remaining index does not entail, as far as possible, an increase of the index level. In addition, the extended index must ensure a sufficiently high selectivity for the query that is no longer supported by its original index. After all, due to the tuning measure, this query cannot use the index tree completely any more.

2.3.5   Low Selectivity of Indexes

This situation frequently occurs when the indexes are not defined carefully enough or for the reason mentioned several times above, namely keeping all accesses free of sorting at any price. The following query showes indexes with low selectivity, recognizable from a relatively small value FULLKEYCARD as compared to the value CARD. FULLKEYCARD indicates the number of different entries in the index, CARD the number of table rows:

```
SELECT
        C.NAME
       ,C.CREATOR
       ,C.TBNAME
       ,C.TBCREATOR
       ,C.FIRSTKEYCARD
```

```
       ,C.FULLKEYCARD
       ,D.CARD
FROM SYSIBM.SYSINDEXES C, SYSIBM.SYSTABLES D
   WHERE C.TBNAME      = D.NAME
       AND C.TBCREATOR   = D.CREATOR
```

Aiming for high
selectivity of the
index

In the case of indexes with low selectivity and, at the same time, large quantities of data, the commands INSERT and DELETE become particularly costly since those indexes have long RID chains. What does this imply for these commands? An index entry that refers to many rows is changed by an INSERT command or a DELETE command. An index is of use, i.e., accelerating accesses, only if the references to the rows, i.e., the record IDs (RID) are sorted. It is exactly this process that takes place in the case of an INSERT or DELETE. The index entry is reorganized. During this time, the index section is locked. Accordingly, no other SQL request is served during this internal processing. You can imagine what happens when such RID chains consist of several thousand entries and these entries are partially deleted. What happens in the case of INSERT is similar: The record ID of the inserted record is included in the RID chain in its sort order.

Including the
timestamp in the
index

A proven means for shortening the RID chains is to lengthen the index by a timestamp field that is filled with the contents of the register CURRENT TIMESTAMP when a row is inserted. When the rows of such a table are accessed, this field is never addressed since its contents are not known anyway and it is of no interest from the application point of view. The selectivity of the index increases greatly by this extension -- this can be easily seen from the contents of the field FULLKEYCARD in the catalog table SYSIBM.SYSINDEXES. At the same time, the internal effort for all INSERT and DELETE commands is reduced. To use even more optimization potential, it should be checked whether the index is even unique after its redesign. In that case, the clause UNIQUE should be specified for CREATE INDEX.

2.4   Excessively Long Runtimes in Batch

For batch operations, the most frequent problem causes can be characterized as follows:

- extensive business,
- too many synchronous IOs,
- processing logic,
- many indexes to a table.

2.4.1   Extensive Business

As already mentioned, extensive business can be a cause for long runtimes. Performance considerations are futile as far as this cause is concerned, unless of course you want to cut the ground from under your feet. However, you could aim to process the extensive business more efficiently.

2.4.2   Too Many Synchronous IOs

In on-line processing, the number of synchronous IOs will normally be relatively high as compared to the number of asynchronous IOs. However, this is usually not serious, because the absolute number of IOs is limited. The situation is different in the case of an extensive batch processing. If the same ratio between synchronous and asynchronous IOs as in on-line processing is maintained, the runtimes will often be too long. Thus, the most important aim for batch operation is to achieve a higher proportion of asynchronous IOs than with on-line processing.

Exploiting Pre-fetch

Technically, this means using to a great extent the properties of the Sequential Pre-fetch and the List Pre-fetch, which are often actually harmful to on-line processing. In on-line processing, owing to the Sequential or List Pre-fetchh, too many rows are internally processed, which are then not required at all by the application in the specific processing unit. Thus, for on-line processing, the absolute number of IOs should be reduced, for instance by using the OPTIMIZE FOR 1 ROW clause, which will switch off only the Pre-fetch without affecting the result set.

Carefully selecting the clustering index

Well, what are the means to increase the proportion of asynchronous IOs? The cure-all that almost always works is using the clustering index. This once again brings us to global physical database design. The index design can be tackled properly only after the likely access types to a table are known, and after frequency and importance of these accesses have been evaluated. The most frequent, or most important, or most time critical access should be supported by the clustering index. Evaluating the access is of primary importance, since only one clustering index is available. You should always keep in mind: the clustering index is a performance index.

By using this index, the number of IOs that are actually performed for providing the data can be reduced by far. This shall be illustrated with an -- admittedly simplified -- example. A given table contains 10 million rows with a record length of 200 bytes. For synchronous processing of this table, assuming 50 milliseconds for a synchronous IO (including the index accesses), about 140 hours of IO time would be required. Whereas, with asynchronous processing with Sequential Prefetchh, for which about 2 milliseconds per page have to be assumed, less than half an hour would be adequate.

To be able to use this index in the manner explained, it is often necessary to design the processing logic differently from that of the on-line processing.

2.4.3   Processing Logic

For application development, it is certainly economical to design functions that are to run both on-line as well as asynchronously just once, and to re-use them. For asynchronous functions with relatively low execution frequency, this procedure is also legitimate.

Caution when using on-line functions in batch

In contrast, functions with high complexity and, at the same time, a high execution frequency require independent design considerations. Examples are monthly invoicing or the annual type-class conversions in the car insurance industry. In these cases, the batch processing cannot be considered to be an order processing system by, in a manner of speaking, building a processing loop around the on-line function. With this design, it is hardly possible to achieve IO reductions by using, for example, a Sequential Pre-fetch. There are several conceivable approaches for such processing.

Sorting input data

The first possible method to use asynchronous processing consists in previously sorting the triggering input data. After being sorted, its sequence should correspond to the sort order of the main processing table. In this way, you achieve usage of the clustering index on this table without physical sorting of the result data.

Another approach is the use of LOAD utilities. Following, a number of possible combinations are discussed.

Using load procedures

The simplest method performs the UPDATE and DELETE operations directly on the table, whereas the INSERT commands are written to a sequential file. If there is no unique key, this data can be uploaded without any difficulty using the LOAD utility with the option RESUME. If there is a requirement for uniqueness, a read operation has to be performed on the table using that key before writing the sequential file. The relieving of the INSERT operations is particularly noticeable when there are several indexes.

REORG after LOAD RESUME

When loading data with the LOAD utility using the RESUME option, the rows which are loaded are added to the end of the table, whereas the index is maintained correctly. Thus, the lines can be well away from their home page, i.e., that page to which they actually belong according to the clustering index. Hence, it is advisable to follow up with a REORG of the table spaces.

Directing SQL statements to sequential files

Another method directs all commands, in principle, to the sequential file. The records to be inserted or modified are written, while the records to be deleted are ignored. Parallel to this processing, the table is unloaded and sorted with the sequential file. The option SORT FIELDS=(....),EQUALS in conjunction with the option SUM FIELDS=NONE is used to reduce duplicate entries, i.e., the updates to a single entry. If the sequential file is the first in the file concatenation of the SORTIN DD instruction, the entry of this file will remain. The SORTOUT file can then be used without difficulty as load data.

Restricting load procedure to one partition

This method is particularly economical when the table to be modified is partitioned -- it is assumed that such is the case with large tables -- and the batch application changes exactly one partition. This is often the case when the tables are clustered with a time-based key and the processing is time-based as well. In this case, there is the option to unload, sort, and load only this partition and to do a full copy afterwards. Elegant as this method may appear to be at first glance, in a production environment, the difficulty is to automatically ensure the correctness of the control statements, especially for the UNLOAD and LOAD step. Here, it proved successful that the processing job itself writes these statements to a file or library, because it knows best which data is currently being processed. With this method, no manual intervention in the job sequence is required.

2.4.4   Too Many Indexes

Another major cause for long batch run times is a high number of indexes to tables that are to be changed. For operational tables, i.e., tables to which INSERT, UPDATE, or DELETE operations are performed, "high" generally means three or more indexes. This can be easily determined from the DB2 catalog with the following query:

```
SELECT
        C.NAME
    ,   C.CREATOR
    , C.DBNAME
    , C.TSNAME
    , COUNT(*)
FROM    SYSIBM.SYSTABLES   C
    , SYSIBM.SYSINDEXES  I
WHERE   C.TYPE       = 'T'
AND     I.TBNAME = C.NAME
AND     I.TBCREATOR = C.CREATOR
GROUP BY
        C.NAME
    , C.CREATOR
    , C.DBNAME
    , C.TSNAME
HAVING COUNT(*) > 3
```

Owing to the fact that many updates have to be performed to the tables, an even higher number of index updates will result. The problem is further intensified by indexes with low selectivity. The selectivity can be read from the DB2 catalog under the entry FULLKEYCARD in the table SYSIBM.SYSINDEXES. If this value is small in relation to the number of rows in the table, the index involved is less selective. Less selective indexes have long RID-chains. Section 2.3 already explained how costly the maintenance of such an index is, and the amount of overhead involved.

The severity of this problem can be reduced by adding more columns to the table or defining a new TIMESTAMP column. In this situation, too, you have to ask yourself whether the index design is correct. Here, correct means that a minimum number of indexes should be present in order to enable proper execution of the SQL requests.

Avoiding redundant indexes

First, it must be checked whether there are any more or less redundant indexes, i.e., indexes that are identical in their first columns and different in their last columns. Mostly, they would have been created to support SQL requests without sorting. At this point, some thought needs to be given as to whether you can put up with sorting as soon as one of the quasi-redundant indexes has been dropped. If the result sets to be sorted are small, this question can mostly be answered in the affirmative.

A solution with a somewhat more complicated sequence is the temporary dropping of indexes. First, you should identify the indexes used by the batch program. They can be easily determined using the DB2 catalog table SYSIBM.SYSPACKDEP. At this point, you have to identify all programs or packages referencing the other indexes of the involved table. These can also be determined using the catalog table mentioned above. On this basis, you will have to generate REBIND control instructions for the concerned packages. After this step, the indexes not required for this step can be dropped and re-created in the next step, but with option DEFER (from DB2 version 3.1). This merely generates the catalog entry of the index, but not the index itself. This only happens when the next LOAD or REORG utility is run. The batch program is run with the remaining indexes required for processing. On completion, the RECOVER INDEX utility is executed so that the indexes previously dropped can be built up again.

Of course, because of its complexity, this method is only suitable for difficult cases that cannot be properly solved in any other way. In any case, it requires a thoroughly tested, complete batch routine. However, as soon as such a routine is available, it can be used in automated mode under production conditions.

There is hope that the problem with indexes will loose some of its more inconvenient aspects with the Type2 indexes of version 4, since this index type will enable "smoother" locking mechanisms.

2.5   Summary

The most important symptoms of performance problems, their technical causes, and the suitable approaches were discussed in this chapter.

Locking problems

Causes: Long Commit intervals
                     Execution of costly operations
                     Hot spots

Measures: Setting Commit points
                     Checkpoint table
                     Reducing INSERT/DELETE
                     High PCTFREE
                     Frequent REORG
                     Using load procedures
                     Reducing the number of indexes
                     Distributing keys
                     Pre-load of tables

Queuing problems

Causes: Similar processing
                     Hot spots

Measures: Distributing keys
                     Pre-load of tables
                     see also: locking problems

"Delivery times instead of response times" in on-line operation

Causes: Too many IOs
                     Sorting large result sets
                     Costly queries
                     Large indexes
                     Low selectivity of indexes

Measures: Using OPTIMIZE FOR
                     Using clustering index
                     Qualifying all conditions
                     No manually programmed joins
                     Checking RUNSTATS

Redundant columns
Pre-load of tables
Simple query formulations
Reducing INDEXLEVEL
No quasi-redundant indexes
Increasing index selectivity

Excessively long runtimes in batch

Causes: Extensive business
Too many synchronous IOs
Processing logic
Many indexes

Measures: Using clustering index
Careful batch design
Combined load procedures
No quasi-redundant indexes
Index-dropping before batch run.

3 Organizational Measures in Software Development

The previous chapter dealt with the most important symptoms and causes of performance problems and presented possible approaches from a technical point of view.

However, in day-to-day practice, it turns out that the same mistakes are made again in the next project if you do not succeed in making performance a "built-in" feature due to the design of the software development process. In the following, organizational measures are pointed out that can significantly reduce the frequency of performance problems.

This chapter will discuss the following topics in detail:

- application scenario and access profile,
- design of critical batch runs,
- access modules,
- reduction of physical data accesses,
- considerations about application architecture,
- standards for software development.

3.1   Application Scenario and Access Profile

To reduce the project risks that become apparent especially in the final phase, it is always advisable to check certain activities as early as possible. This is a general rule of action that applies universally, but is unfortunately followed all too seldom.

Let us put these rules in more concrete terms.

Projects of a certain size can be assumed to be managed with the help of a procedure model. The central task of a procedure model is to standardize the software development process.

What is the procedure model made up of? The most significant terms are phase, activity, and result. The phases with their respective activities are planned; the results obtained therefrom are quality-assured. The basic assumption of the popular procedure models is a development process with stepwise refinement -- top-down. Starting from global descriptions, increasingly detailed results are achieved in the defined activities. Normally, quality assurance measures are taken at the end of a phase for the results produced.

Performance problems occur nonetheless. From experience, this is because quality assurance concentrates more on formalisms and business-related topics of the documentation than on technical concerns. In other words: the usual quality assurance measures still remain sensible and necessary, but they must be supplemented by additional checks related to the technical environment. So, where should measures be taken to reduce the likelihood of subsequent performance problems?

Collecting quantities at an early stage

An aspect already mentioned in the context of procedure models -- it cannot be repeated often enough -- is the proven fact that the earlier a modification or a correction is made, the cheaper it is. For our purposes, this means -- for each phase of a project -- to collect as much information on performance as possible, to discuss it with qualified authorities in-house, and, possibly, to plan or to execute first measures. These measures can be of totally different types. Both the revision of the results that have been just obtained, as well as early hardware ordering are conceivable here.

The thought behind this approach is that already in the phases in which no implementation takes place, certain activities have to be performed that make a statement about performance aspects.

3.1.1   Application Scenario

In the early phases in which the business rough design and the business fine design is worked out, information about the expected load needs to be collected. This information should be based on the technical units of measurement such as the business transactions or procedures. For in most cases, the methods staff who have themselves never done project work, but who define the procedure model, advocate the opinion that such things are completely out of place in a phase in which the future system is to be described from the business point of view. Erroneously, it is assumed that the business design only consists of the data model, the function model, and the process model. Another dimension of the business design is, however, the quantities that have to be processed by the future application system. At this point, the first measure comes in to clarify performance aspects already in the business design. For an interactive system, this means to collect the quantities per business transaction or procedure to be handled. In the following, the achieved result is called the application scenario. Astounding results were obtained in a number of application systems in which the application scenario was made out later. The quantities that the system would have had to process in the given environment were too high for the existing machine to handle. With this information available at the time of the fine design, suitable steps could have been planned or set on foot already in this project phase.

For an application scenario sample refer to section 6.3.

Naturally, in those project phases in which the DP design and the implementation take place, there are also other activities in which more detailed statements about performance are compiled. In the following, this information is classified under the term access profile.

3.1.2   Access Profile

Access paths
in case of joins

The core statement of the access profile is that the developer must describe his conception as to how the database system should access the data with the given physical database design. For accesses to only one table, this is almost trivial, because the number of pages to be read can be derived from the type of index support. In commercial systems, however, such an access is not the rule. Normally, SQL joins are used to access the required data. Severe problems may occur if the linkage of the tables is either not supported by indexes or if there are excessively large result sets for the first table. In these cases, a great number of synchronous IOs, i.e., long processing time as well, is to be expected. If the planned access paths are already documented in this form in the DP design phase -- and therefore are also transparent -- then, if required, design changes are possible with relatively modest effort.

The other advantage is that with the access profile you define the "measuring staff" for the future application system. This aspect is illustrated in somewhat more detail here. After the introduction of an application system, different opinions occur between the supplier and the buyer regarding the quality of the system with respect to its response times. The so-called "delivery times" in the case of somewhat extensive transactions are criticized. The access profile provides, at a very early stage in the development process, the opportunity to discuss and define the effects of demanding business-related requirements with the future users. It may be quite sensible to design a transaction with powerful business-related functionality and equally utilizing lots of computer resources in order to achieve a high degree of business utility. However, you should not cherish the illusion that such a transaction has response times just as short as another one that is significantly less expensive. Access profile can reduce the risk of unrealistic expectations of the users.

3.2   Design of Critical Batch Runs

Batch requires a
separate design

To save effort and time in projects, some project leaders try to save on an independent design of batch runs despite knowing that extensive processing is to take place in these batch runs. Instead of an independent design tailored to the processing and the table structure -- details will be presented later -- an attempt is made to re-use similar on-line processing procedures by simply placing a control loop around the basic processing in the dialog. Initially, this approach seems to be advantageous for the project because hardly any separate effort would need to be planned for the batch part of the project. In particular, testing would presumably not be required. Time reveals, however, that this is a naive miscalculation. The batch runtimes become exorbitantly long; these jobs not only need too many resources, but are simply not executable any more since they have the additional adverse effect of hindering other applications as well.

Example for
execution times

This is illustrated with the following example. The starting point is an interactive processing that opens, reads, and closes five cursors. Each of these cursors has such a small result set -- which, in addition, is supported by a clustering index -- that the data of each cursor is located on one page. The tables and hence the indexes are each so large that the index leaf pages and the table space pages are usually not located in the buffer pool. With normal system behavior and the correct setting of the buffer pool, it can be assumed that the root page and the intermediate pages of each index are located in the buffer pool. Accordingly, five synchronous accesses to the index leaf pages and five synchronous accesses to the data pages are required for data provision. There are ten synchronous accesses with 25 milliseconds each amounting to 0.250 seconds. For an on-line application, this is, if not an excellent value, definitely a tenable value considering the processing involved.

It can be very easily shown that very long execution times may result for a batch which processes not one but many access keys according to this logic.

Number of Executions	IO Time per Execution	Total Time in Seconds	Total Time in Hours
100	0.250	25	0.007
1,000	0.250	250	0.069
10,000	0.250	2,500	0.694
100,000	0.250	25,000	6.944
1,000,000	0.250	250,000	69.444
10,000,000	0.250	2,500,000	694.444

This example illustrates that a batch process behaving like an on-line application can process 100,000 access keys only to a limited extent, but that access keys in excess of that cannot be realistically processed. Projects that followed the procedure described above made this experience -- although only just before their introduction. A simple estimate of the execution times would have made this result clear much earlier, but the planners were either not ready or able to do it. The expected saving of effort had now to be achieved in a much shorter time; in addition, the introduction of the batch components became more expensive than it would have been with normal planning. So, what is to be done?

3.2.1   Using Prefetch

With extensive batch functions, it is a particularly good idea to use the prefetch property for processing. Prefetch should be avoided in on-line processing -- it causes DB2 to fetch far too much data internally, which results in increased IO and CPU times -- but is a desirable factor in batch processing. Since in such a processing a considerable part of the tables needs to be processed -- regardless of whether a pure read-only functionality, e.g., for statistics, is involved, or an update functionality -- it is favorable to provide data in an asynchronous process.

This is illustrated with the following example. In one unit of work, a given process has to read data for one access key from three tables. `Table1` has 3 million rows of 300 bytes each, thus 13 rows per data page. `Table2` has 5 million rows of 200 bytes each, i.e., 20 rows per page; and `Table3` consists of 15 million rows of 100 bytes each, thus 40 rows per page. In one processing unit, a single `SELECT` is issued on `Table1`. On `Table2`, one cursor is processed with an average result set of two rows, which are normally located on one page. On Table3, one cursor is processed with an average result set of 5 rows. Thus, a simplified assumption can be made that both single SELECT as well as cursors require about 50 milliseconds per execution; i.e., 25 milliseconds for retrieving the index leaf page and 25 milliseconds for the table space page. Given this table size, both pages are normally not located in the buffer pool. Thus, for single processing, as it is given in on-line operation, an average IO time of 150 milliseconds per unit of work would be required. If 500,000 units of work have to be carried out in a batch processing, this would result in an IO time of about 21 hours. Elapsed times like this are absolutely not acceptable, except for a one-time data migration.

Using prefetch

In contrast, if the processing control is modified to sequentially read the three tables with a cursor that accesses via the clustering index and uses sequential prefetch, then the resulting IO times are completely different. It is easily recalculated that providing one page requires an average of 2 milliseconds when using sequential prefetch. Accordingly, about 230,000 pages from Table1, 250,000 from Table2, and 375,000 from Table3 are processed. Thus, for completely processing the total of 855,000 pages with 2 milliseconds of IO time required for each page, a total IO time of 1,710 seconds would result. This is less than half an hour as compared to the above 21 hours.

For more transparency, this example is shown in simplified SQL notation.

Variant 1: Single Processing without Prefetch

```
DECLARE cursor-table2 CURSOR FOR
  SELECT ...
  FROM  table2 T2
  WHERE T2.keyfield = :value-from-control-file
  ORDER BY T2.keyfield, ...

DECLARE cursor-table3 CURSOR FOR
  SELECT ...
  FROM table3 T3
  WHERE T3.keyfield = :value-from-control-file
  ORDER BY T2.keyfield, ...


Reading control file
PERFORM loop UNTIL end-of-control-file
```

```
SELECT ...
FROM table1 T1
WHERE T1.keyfield = :value-from-control-file

OPEN cursor-table2
FETCH cursor-table2
PERFORM loop-T2 UNTIL SQLCODE = 100
    Processing table2
    FETCH cursor-table2
END-PERFORM
CLOSE cursor-table2

OPEN cursor-table3
FETCH cursor-table3
PERFORM loop-T3 UNTIL SQLCODE = 100
    Processing table3
    FETCH cursor-table3
END-PERFORM
CLOSE cursor-table3

Reading control file

END-PERFORM
```

Variant 2: Sequential Processing with Prefetch

```
DECLARE cursor-table1 CURSOR FOR
SELECT ...
FROM table1 T1
ORDER BY T1.keyfield

DECLARE cursor-table2 CURSOR FOR

SELECT ...
FROM table2 T2
ORDER BY T2.keyfield, ...
DECLARE cursor-table3 CURSOR FOR
SELECT ...
FROM table3 T3
ORDER BY T3.keyfield, ...

OPEN cursor-table1
```

```
OPEN cursor-table2
OPEN cursor-table3

FETCH cursor-table1
FETCH cursor-table2
FETCH cursor-table2


Reading control file

PERFORM loop UNTIL end-of-control-file

   PERFORM loop-T2 UNTIL
           change-value-from-control-file
           OR SQLCODE = 100
      IF T2.keyfield = value-from-control-file
         Processing table2
      END-IF
      FETCH cursor-table2
   END-PERFORM
   PERFORM loop-T3 UNTIL
           change-value-from-control-file
           OR SQLCODE = 100
      IF T3.keyfield = value-from-control-file
         Processing table3
      END-IF
      FETCH cursor-table3
   END-PERFORM

   FETCH cursor-table1
   Reading control file

END-PERFORM

CLOSE cursor-table1
CLOSE cursor-table2
CLOSE cursor-table3
```

Note that in variant 2, no restrictive WHERE condition is formulated in the three cursors; instead, the tables are read completely. In this case, the filtering as to whether a row being read is to be processed, is done -- exceptionally -- in the program.

Further, the cursors are opened and closed just once. If, for increasing competing accesses, shorter COMMIT points than the

execution time of the program are required, there are two possibilities.

The first option is to formulate all cursors with the clause WITH
HOLD. Thus, they will remain positioned even in a COMMIT
command, and reading can be continued without requiring any
further measures. However, this clause can result in some
small system overhead.

In the second option, something has to be done to the cursor
definition as well as to the program logic. The cursors include a
matching condition as shown below:

```
SELECT ...
FROM    table1 T1
WHERE
        T1.keyfield > :restart-key
ORDER BY
        T1.keyfield, ...
```

Performing
COMMIT at regular
intervals

As with the first option, the program issues a COMMIT command
at specific times. At the same time, the current access key that
was completely processed prior to the COMMIT command is
saved. After the COMMIT command, all the cursors are reopened and processing can continue as hitherto.

It is more or less a matter of taste which of the two options you
select. It is important, though, that one of these options is used
throughout. For this purpose, it is a good idea to provide standard solutions for application development. This is best done
by the DBA group in cooperation with the group that is responsible for methods and tools.

Another option for drastically reducing long runtimes of batch
programs is to use load utilities. These will be explained below.

3.2.2   Load Procedure

We distinguish two types of load procedures according to the
options of the DB2 LOAD utilities:

- Procedure with Load Replace,

- Procedure with Load Resume.

LOAD REPLACE

Let us first consider the procedure with Load Replace. This
procedure uses the following control statement of the load utility:

```
LOAD DATA
    . . .
    REPLACE
    LOG NO
    INTO TABLE table
```

In the case of partitioned table spaces, it is further possible to load selectively into a partition:

```
LOAD DATA
    . . .
    LOG NO
    INTO TABLE table
    PART n REPLACE
```

SQL statements
are replaced

As compared to a pure SQL procedure, in which all INSERT, UPDATE, and DELETE statements are directly executed with SQL, in the case of a Load procedure, the batch program has to be modified as follows for these statements.

All INSERT statements are replaced by a WRITE command that acts on a sequential file. To optimize the execution time of the batch program, a high blocking factor should be set for this file so that the number of physical IOs is reduced. The background for this step is that the physical IOs are proportionally dependent on the block size and number of buffers.

If the batch program includes UPDATE statements these will be re-directed, like the INSERT statements, to the sequential file using the same WRITE command.

The replace procedure provides two options for handling DELETE statements:

One option is to maintain the DELETE statements unchanged as compared to the pure SQL procedure. This is the simplest solution regarding procedure changes. Since the DELETE statement is one of the costly SQL statements -- after all, relatively many actions are required on the table space and, in particular, on the existing indexes -- this can lead to further problems, particularly in the case of tables with a great many indexes and, simultaneously, many DELETE operations. This will not only manifest itself in increased execution times, but also result in locking conflicts on the secondary indexes.

**Replacing
DELETE
statements by
UPDATE
statements**

Therefore, specifically in the case of tables with multiple in-dexes, the other option should be considered, i.e., substituting the DELETE statements with UPDATE statements. In this vari-ant, the table is expanded by a delete flag with two values. This flag can be defined, for instance, as a field of data type CHAR(01) and the range {' ', 'D'}. When INSERTing a row into the table, this flag is blank. Now, an UPDATE state-ment on this delete flag is executed instead of a DELETE statement:

```
EXEC SQL
    UPDATE table
        SET delete-flag = 'D'
    WHERE condition
END-EXEC
```

**Delete flags should
not be a part of the
index**

In this step, care must be taken that the delete flag is not in-cluded in any index as far as possible, so that updating is re-quired on the table space page exclusively. The corresponding step on the SELECT side is to supplement all WHERE conditions in the SELECT statement with the clause

```
AND delete-flag = ' '
```

**Regular
reorganization**

This procedure is completed by a regular clean-up of the logi-cally deleted rows. This is best done by unloading the table with the following SELECT statement:

```
SELECT *
FROM    table
WHERE   delete-flag = ' '
```

The unloaded data is then sorted and re-loaded into the table with the option REPLACE. Then, you should run a backup, a RUNSTATS, and a rebind of the concerned packages.

These are the changes which are to be carried out to the batch program as compared to the pure SQL procedure. Let us now consider the general sequence of the load procedure with Load Replace.

First, the modified batch program is run, which writes the INSERT and DELETE statements to a sequential file. In paral-lel, you can already unload the table or one of its partitions.

The next step in this sequence consists of sorting the load file from the batch program with the unload file of the DB2 utility. A sample job control would read as follows:

```
//SORT       EXEC SORT
//SORTIN     DD DISP=SHR,DSN=load-file
//           DD DISP=SHR,DSN=unload-file
//SORTOUT    DD DISP=SHR,DSN=sort-output
//SYSIN      DD *
  SORT FIELDS=(start,length,CH,A)
  SUM FIELDS=NONE
```

This sample job control is applicable to such load files from the batch program to which no UPDATE rows have been written. In this case, no duplicates of the sort fields can occur. If the load file does contain UPDATE rows, this job control should be modified as follows:

```
//SORT       EXEC SORT
//SORTIN     DD DISP=SHR,DSN=load-file
//           DD DISP=SHR,DSN=unload-file
//SORTOUT    DD DISP=SHR,DSN=sort-output
//SYSIN      DD *
  SORT FIELDS=(start,length,CH,A),EQUALS
  SUM FIELDS=NONE
```

Sorting with EQUALS option

The SORT FIELDS statement differs by the EQUALS option. If there are multiple occurrences of the contents of the sort fields, this option maintains the sequence in which the records were read. By mentioning the load file first in the SORTIN concatenation, the UPDATE record takes the first position. The clause SUM FIELDS=NONE results in only the first record of duplicate keys being written to the output. Thus, the table contains the unchanged records of the table (from the unload file), the new records (from the load file), and the modified records (also from the load file). The table can then be re-loaded with the output of the sort utility. Of course, the option REPLACE is used in the load utility,

This procedure is completed with a FULL COPY, a RUNSTATS, and the REBINDs of the affected packages.

Let us now consider the LOAD RESUME procedure.

LOAD RESUME

As compared to the LOAD REPLACE procedure, which can process all the modifications to a table by INSERT, UPDATE, and

DELETE statements, the procedure with LOAD RESUME provides somewhat less flexibility. But on the other hand, some steps can be omitted.

Replacing INSERT statements

As in the procedure with Load Replace, the INSERT operations can be replaced by WRITE commands to a sequential file. For UPDATE and DELETE commands, however, this is not possible. In this procedure, there is no intermediate program or utility available to reduce duplicate records to the one correct record, or to eliminate records to be deleted. Therefore, in the LOAD RESUME procedure, the SQL statements UPDATE and DELETE must remain unchanged in the application program. In the case of applications that frequently use these operations as compared to the INSERTs, it is in doubt whether this procedure is at all worthwhile. In the case of applications that mainly execute INSERT operations, this procedure can still be worthwhile. Prior to loading the new insertions into the table, two things should happen: Sorting the data according to the clustering index and, as a precaution, a FULL COPY of the table. Should the load process be aborted because of problems, the table can be restored in the shortest possible time on the basis of the FULL COPY, if there is no alternative for repairing the table.

After successful execution of the load utility, a new FULL COPY should be run for security reasons prior to any further changes to the table.

Deterioration of the CLUSTERRATIO

In contrast to the procedure with Load Replace, the organization degree of the table, as can be read from the CLUSTERRATIO, becomes continuously worse in this procedure since the new rows are appended to the end of the table. Hence, a REORG should be run for this table at regular intervals in order to avoid any deterioration in the response times for interactive processing. In the procedure with Load Replace, reorganization is done implicitly in the sorting step.

In this respect, some thought needs to be given to whether, on a long-term basis, the REPLACE procedure actually needs just as much effort and machine time as the RESUME procedure. At first glance, the REPLACE procedure appears to require more effort. Direct calculation formulae for the comparison of the two procedures cannot be given here, since the times required depend on several influencing factors. These factors include the table size, the modification rate, the relation between INSERT operations on the one hand and the UPDATE and DELETE operations on the other, as well as the frequency of the batch run.

Finally it can be stated for the different batch processes that these independent design considerations can result in considerable savings in machine time. Hence, it is a good idea to take organizational measures to ensure that this aspect is taken into account on project planning. Proven means to achieving this are to integrate this point into the procedure model as well as to perform quality assurance activities on the project plans.

3.3   Access Modules

Another organizational measure to design a more efficient database usage is the definition of access modules per entity from the conceptual data model or, for 1:1 mappings, per table. This shall be illustrated starting with two examples from various projects.

Example without table access module

In a partner management system, personal data and address data was stored in different tables. The address table also included the historical data. One of the standard accesses was a join of the personal data with the relevant current address data. Historical address data was read only in exceptional cases with exactly one transaction.

During a tuning project, these accesses to the partner management system appeared in the hit list of costly accesses. The tuning measure taken was to split the address data in such a way that the current data was integrated in the personal data and only historical data was kept in the address table. Despite a slightly increased maintenance effort for archiving the address data, the standard access to the partner data became much faster, since joins were no longer required.

The problem with this solution was that all accesses to the partner data were scattered in many different programs. To achieve the aspired solution, all the relevant programs had to be changed. It is obvious that this solution -- which was, in fact, implemented in the end -- was really costly. Usage of data access modules would have avoided a considerable effort.

Let's take a look at the second example. In this system, in which payment transaction data is processed, there existed the entities "debit entry" and "payment item", each of which has a huge data volume of about 80 million rows each due to extensive business. To achieve higher parallelism and processing independence, and smaller units for the REORG and LOAD utilities, the tables were partitioned -- partially with new, artificial keys -- as well as split into different tables according to business-related criteria. By using data access modules that completely encapsulated these technical measures to the application programs, it was possible to benefit from a number of advantages.

Encapsulation of technical measures

The complete encapsulation of the technical measures provides the option, for the future as well, to be able to carry out the necessary technical modifications (such as further splitting into different tables, or modifications to the routine for determining the artificial partitioning key) with relatively low programming effort. Were the accesses to the resultant tables of the business entity not encapsulated, there would be hardly any realistic chance for subsequent changes.

Such a data access module should provide at least the standard accesses to an entity. The scope can be described as follows:

Standard functionality of data access modules

- INSERT, UPDATE, DELETE one row

- If the unique key consists of several columns, the UPDATE and DELETE commands which act on generic keys should be provided.

- Single SELECT via the unique key

- The following cursors should be defined: Access via all the generic keys of the primary key and of all the secondary keys with suitable ORDER BY clauses.

For each cursor that is defined, all possible command combinations must be provided:

- OPEN Cursor

- OPEN, FETCH with the desired number of fetches

- OPEN, FETCH with the desired number of fetches, CLOSE

- FETCH with the desired number of fetches

- FETCH with the desired number of fetches, CLOSE

- CLOSE Cursor

Macro techniques may be used to provide all the functions of a cursor. With these standard functions being provided, it is possible, from experience, to cover 90% of all the accesses to a table. For the application developers in a project, this method has the advantage that in case of complex implementations they do not have to bother with single details, but can concentrate on the business-related requirements. They are provided with a call interface to the data access module, and hence to the tables. This significantly contributes to the productivity of a developer. Similarly, the testing effort is also reduced. The data access module can be tested stand-alone, and then be made available to the project. Subsequently, only the correctness of the call to this module needs to be checked.

Since such a module is written by exactly one team member, that person is deeply involved in the subject matter. This also results in certain productivity advantages.

Owing to the possibility of re-using such a module -- this does not only apply within an application system, but, in central systems such as contract management or partner management systems, even across systems -- an overall application also becomes much better structured and hence also easier to expand and to maintain.

A special regulation has to be set for SQL joins between tables. The option here is to assign the join, according to business criteria, to such a data access module.

One last technical advantage must be mentioned, despite this chapter's predominantly organizational considerations. Owing to the separation of the business-related code and data accesses, the number of packages is reduced. With smaller and, more particularly, re-usable packages, the system overhead can be noticeably reduced by better thread-reuse.

3.4   Reducing Data Accesses

So far, this chapter essentially presented measures to minimize the locking of resources and synchronous IOs.

Over and above these measures, infrastructural measures can also provide the facility to avoid data accesses. If the interactive programs are compatible with each other, and if they are combined based on their individual functionality for processing business transactions, i.e., a business-related unit of work, data is normally read at the start of a business transaction and is further required in the modules which are subsequently called. The argument of function encapsulation could be used to justify that, on principle, each program reads all its required data by itself or requests for it by calling another program. Although programs do become independent with this method, there is also an unnecessary overhead involved.

Passing fields through

Without introducing restrictions on encapsulation, it proved advantageous to build optimizations into the programs. This can be done by defining a reserved area for frequently used fields in the application within the CICS COMMAREA. This area is passed through an application system in an application-specific manner. By marking it at a specific fixed location, this part of the COMMAREA can even be used system-wide. Now, if a program detects that it can "understand", i.e., interpret that application-specific area, it can use that data. For example, the relevant current access keys with attributes which apply across module boundaries are stored in this area. Also, in each interactive program, there is a routine which evaluates this area and, on that basis, requests the data related to the access keys to be processed only if required, i.e., only if the area is empty. This standard functionality will avoid lots of data accesses.

One more word regarding COMMAREA. It could be argued that the application-specific area should be made as large as possible in order to avoid additional data accesses. As long as the COMMAREA is restricted to a maximum of 4K, no negative effects will be noticeable. The enlargement of the COMMAREA from 4K to 32K should be avoided under any circumstances for performance reasons.

3.5   Considerations Regarding the Application Architecture

As already mentioned in the previous section, the introduction of certain standards regarding data accesses is to be advocated from the performance point of view. In addition to the measures for avoiding data accesses discussed previously, there are also other areas in which standardization not only has positive effects on the quality of the application but on their performance, too.

Implementing central functionalities as services

To have any chance at all of being able to optimize central functionalities with a tenable effort, these functionalities must be strictly separated from the actual application functions. This is best done with such an encapsulation that these central functions are invoked via CALL. This solution is more flexible than encapsulation using macros. Since macros are integrated in the actual application code by a preprocessor run, modification of a central function will necessitate new preprocessor runs followed by Compile, Link, and Bind, for all the application programs which use this macro. As long as the data interface of the central function does not change, the solution with the CALL interface necessitates no further action.

Only with such an encapsulation, you are in a position to optimize the central function. And these very functions have the biggest potential for improvement, since they are generally called very frequently.

As examples, the following areas can be nominated as candidates for such central functions:

- controlling of procedures/business transactions,

- printing services,

- authorization services.

Even functionalities such as the automatic assignment of access keys are to be included in this category.

3.6   Standards for Software Development

Specifications regarding performance aspects should be included in the suitable standards for the software development so that a large part of the later performance problems can be avoided.

3.6.1   Programming Guidelines

Among the most important of the specifications for the software development process are the programming guidelines. Nowadays they often cover only naming conventions, permitted commands in programming languages, specifications on structured programming, standards for error handling, and restart procedures. The specifications on these complex topics are important and necessary for a reliable quality of the software being developed. As long as processing of mainly sequential or VSAM files was involved, they did cover the most important areas. As soon as database processing comes into play, they continue to be required, but are not sufficient for high software quality, since completely new classes of problems for application development emerge from using databases. Hence, it is necessary to supplement the previous standards with topics related to database processing. One approach that has proved successful in quite a number of companies with many years of intensive DB2 usage is the preparation of a DB2 manual.

3.6.2   DB2 Manual

Such a manual addresses the application development group and describes how to use DB2 in their software systems. For usability reasons it should not just exist in printed form, but as far as possible be also available on-line. This ensures that it can be used without any significant additional effort during software development. Incidentally, this also prevents excuses such as "I wasn't aware of that" and "It's not possible to refer to it anyway".

How should such a DB2 manual be structured? The following is an example of a possible structure:

- Fundamentals on DB2 and SQL

- Introduction to the operation mode of the DB2 Optimizer; explanations of the terms stage 1, stage 2, indexable

- Functioning of joins

- Permitted SQL commands

- Forbidden SQL commands

- Parallel processing and its involved locking problems

- Working with access profiles

- Performance considerations for batch processing.

3.7   Using Quality Assurance Tools

Comprehensive
QA coverage only
with tool

Nothing further needs to be said here about the basic importance of quality assurance in the DB2 area. The early involvement of DBAs in the project will certainly have a positive effect
on the quality of the application system being developed. For
larger projects, however, it will probably be impossible -- for ca-
pacity reasons -- to keep up with this measure. In such a situation, quality assurance will be confined to random samples.
The use of suitable tools is indispensable for extensive quality
assurance.

Integration in the
development
process

However, the approach should not be to take quality assurance
measures only at the end of programming. Rather, they should
be integrated in the development process in such a way that by
using the tools, quality is built into the application system. As a
result, these tools have to meet certain additional requirements.

Let us therefore consider the requirements that must be met by
QA tools, both from the point of view of software development
as well as of the DBA group. The requirements can be divided
into the categories

- static quality requirements on programs,

- dynamic quality requirements on programs,

- usability requirements on the QA tool.

3.7.1   Static Quality Requirements

Checks on the
source code

By this category, checks are understood which can be performed by the QA tool without having to refer to catalog information such as the size of the tables or defined indexes. The
tool should be able to perform the following checks:

- No SELECT * in application programs

SELECT *

Apart from the higher expense at runtime as compared to an
SQL statement with only the necessary fields being qualified
in the SELECT list, experience shows that using SELECT *
may cause problems when expanding tables with additional
fields. Since the provided fields no longer correspond to the
list of host variables in the INTO clause, modifications to tables will also entail a program modification. When using an
explicit SELECT list, an application program will be able to
continue to run without modifications even after the expan-
sion of tables with new fields.

- No usage of WHENEVER

WHENEVER

When using WHENEVER, there is no possibility to trap the INSERT of duplicate keys into a table on the program side. For reasons of efficiency, instead of a previous read, it may be advisable to first attempt an INSERT and, on failure, to perform an UPDATE.

Another point against using the WHENEVER clause is checking whether certain keys are present in the table. As compared to a cursor, a single SELECT is more efficient. However, if the hit list consists of several records, the program branches to the WHENEVER routine due to SQLCODE -811.

Referential integrity

One last argument against using WHENEVER is the use of RI (referential integrity). Here too, there are a number of negative SQLCODES that have to be trapped programmatically.

- Ban on unnecessary arithmetic in SQL statements

Arithmetic in SQL statements

Arithmetic in SQL statements prevents index usage in many cases.

One example for unnecessary arithmetic is the following clause:

```
WHERE column1 = :host-var + 6
```

In contrast, the following example is permitted, since there is no alternative formulation:

```
WHERE column1 = column2 + 6
```

- No usage of the SQL components DDL and DCL in application programs

DDL
DCL

The SQL components DDL (Data Definition Language) with commands such as CREATE TABLE, and DCL (Data Control Language) with commands such as GRANT or REVOKE, should not normally be used in application systems, since their usage can result in unpredictable locking activities on the DB2 catalog. One exception would be, for example, a system that provides a user interface for the commands mentioned to certain authorities in the company.

- No qualification of the CREATOR in the application program

CREATOR

Qualifying of the CREATOR in SQL statements in the form

```
SELECT ...
FROM    creator.table
WHERE ...
```

will necessitate a program modification when the program is transferred from one environment to another, e.g., from the development environment to the production environment, since the tables are usually created by different UserIDs. This modification is less efficient and a source of unnecessary errors.

- Specification of the column names for INSERT statements

As is the case when specifying an explicit SELECT list, the field list of the inserted values must be explicitly specified for the INSERT statement in order to be independent from table expansions. In addition, the statement is better documented by specifying the column names.

Additional checks are possible, depending on company-specific standards such as naming conventions. For ease of use, it must be possible to switch these checks on and off.

Let's now tackle the dynamic quality requirements on programs.

3.7.2   Dynamic Quality Requirements

This category includes the requirements that cannot be met by merely knowing the source code of an application program, but require information from the program environment as well. From experience, the following checks are suitable for increasing the quality:

- Correspondence between the definition of the table columns and the host variables.

No usage of
existing indexes

On discordance, there is the risk that the Optimizer will not consider suitable existing indexes when determining the access path.

One variant of this case is different formats of table columns that are used to connect several tables in one join.

- Different evaluation factors for canceling automatic checking

It is obvious that the resource consumption of on-line and batch programs has to be assessed differently. A QA tool must be flexible enough to allow those thresholds to be adjusted differently.

- Checking the EXPLAIN against access profiles

When working with access profiles, it is advisable to compare them with the EXPLAIN results. The tool should comprise at least a user-exit for activating company-specific routines.

Access profile
EXPLAIN

• Evaluation of an SQL statement based on a cost factor

Cost factor

Like the evaluation of a statement by the Optimizer, the individual SQL statements should be evaluated and balanced with cost factors. These results are the basis for the decision of the tool, whether or not to continue further checking of the application program.

• Indications on the access quality

Indexable
Stage1
Stage2

For the WHERE clauses of a query, the Administration Guide provides information on how indexes are used for the access path, and in which DB2 component processing takes place. The terms "indexable", "Stage1", and "Stage2" can be mentioned in this context. With these evaluations, the expense of an SQL statement at runtime can be determined. It is very helpful when a QA tool makes SQL statements transparent in this respect.

• Archiving the PLAN_TABLE

The access quality can be determined by using the PLAN_TABLE. Changes assume, however, that this information is archived with the EXPLAIN statement and therefore can be evaluated.

• Highlighting accesses caused by RI (referential integrity).

Referential
integrity

A QA tool should provide the possibility to highlight particularly those SQL statements internally induced at runtime due to using RI. The additional expense that is caused, for instance by the DELETE CASCADE, can be significant. This argument should be considered particularly for the fact that the information about induced SQL statements cannot be obtained from the EXPLAIN.

As with the criteria for static quality, additional company-specific checking is conceivable here as well.

3.7.3   Usability Requirements on the QA Tool

It is important that a QA tool is a natural component of the software development process in order to ensure being of the most possible use. This already determines its most important types of usage:

- interactive in the software development environment
- embedding in compile procedures.

As already mentioned, it is important that the QA tool is not used at the end of the development process, but during the work on an application program.

Interactive test of the SQL statement

In an optimum situation, a software developer is able to interactively evaluate his SQL statements by the QA tool right when working on the source code and therefore is able to continuously improve his statements. For more complicated topics, a DBA would be available in the background. It must be stated, however, that such a tool will relieve the DBA of many time-consuming activities. By using the tool, quality is built straight into the application systems.

Embedding in compile procedures

Regardless of its interactive usage during program generation, it must be possible to embed a component in the various compile procedures. A preprocessor step, which is run before the actual program compilation proved effective in this respect. Due to the return code, the program may not be compiled at all. But here too, it is suitable that checks are not implemented rigidly but are configurable instead. Also conceivable is an exception table containing certain program names so that no checking is done for these programs.

With all the emphasis on quality thinking, flexibility of the QA tool should not be underestimated, so that it does not hinder the development process. Only then users will accept it and use it.

4 Case Studies

The preceding chapters treated both the technical causes including approaches for solutions of performance problems and the organizational measures to reduce the hazard of such problems. This chapter gets on with the practice.

It discusses several case studies from "real life" in detail. Each case study is internally structured in initial situation, potential problems with prime importance, and the approach which in practice already met with success.

In detail, these case studies treat the following subjects:

- queues of transactions in on-line operation,

- avoidance of hot-spots,

- effects of non-uniform distribution of attribute values in case of joins,

- special Optimizer features when formulating restart keys in cursors,

- reducing asynchronous IOs in case of hierarchical structures,

- comparison of `LOAD` and `INSERT` techniques.

4.1   Queues in On-line Operation

4.1.1   Initial Situation

This case study describes a typical infrastructure problem.

Lock table

In a project, a central lock table is to be implemented for the various business objects as "customer" or "contract" together with their respective access keys, i.e., the lock terms.

A simple solution of this problem is a central lock table that might initially look as follows:

Lock Type	Lock Key
Customer	4711
Customer	5813
Contract	G2603
Contract	YV0AA
Invoice	96/114
Voucher	1996/11/21,110341
...	...

The lock type specifies the business object to be locked. This lock table does not store the information as to which tables a particular lock refers to. The application must completely contain the related logic. On each modification of a contract, for instance, each application function that is able to process contracts has to check whether its intended modifications overlap with lock table entries.

In order to enable the storage of the structural different access keys of the various business objects in one field, this field must not be defined data-type-specifically. Fundamentally, an access key to a table can have every valid format and further can be composed of several fields. Therefore, the key information in the lock table is defined as a character string. Consequently, the key structure must be interpreted in the application.

A unique key on this table, consisting of the fields `lock type` and `lock key`, enables automatic recognition of concurrent locking attempts on a business object.

With this basic information, a lock on a business object can simply be controlled.

All functions utilizing this form of lock technique must start with an access to this lock table as soon as their own access key is known. Since the function does not only want to merely check whether it can work on this object but wants to execute the modification, it will start attempting to INSERT the application object, for example the lock type "contract" with its identification, i.e., the lock key 4711.

This action establishes an exclusive lock on the related page. This lock is held until the next COMMIT point: an EXEC SQL COMMIT command in batch or a SYNCPOINT in a CICS dialog. After this, the lock entry is available in the table, and the corresponding page lock is released. At the end of the business unit of work, a DELETE command removes the lock entry from the table. For the duration of this instruction an exclusive lock is established as well, which will be removed at the next COMMIT point as described above.

Scenarios for concurrent access

For a concurrent function, i.e., a function that wants to change the same access key of the same business object, the following four situations may occur:

1. The concurrent function tries to insert its lock term while the first function still holds the lock caused by an INSERT. In this case, the second function enters a wait loop that will be terminated either through a time-out (SQLCODE -911 or -913), or through a duplicate key, (SQLCODE -803).

2. The first function has already released its lock on the inserted row through a COMMIT command. The second function immediately encounters a duplicate key with SQLCODE -803.

3. The first function maintains an exclusive lock on the lock term caused by the DELETE command. In this case, the second function enters a wait loop that will be terminated either through a time-out (SQLCODE -911 or -913), or through a duplicate key (SQLCODE -803).

4. The first function has already committed its DELETE on the lock term, i.e., released its lock. Thus, the second function's INSERT is immediately successful. This means as well, that both functions are executed in sequence, that they are no longer concurrent.

In all situations ending with a negative SQLCODE for the second function, the second function has to be terminated for the moment. Its execution can be attempted again later.

This shows the completeness of this simple construction of a business lock. Let's go on considering the problems that can occur with this lock functionality.

4.1.2   Problem Description

Too many locks on table spaces and indexes

One of the most important problems is the occurrence of a great number of locks. Until version 3.1 inclusive, the smallest lock unit is one page. That means that all entries available in the page are locked until the next COMMIT command. Compared with locks on table space pages, locks on the index pages caused by an INSERT or DELETE command are considerable more serious. From Version 4.1 onwards it is possible to reduce the lock unit for one table space to one row. This might avoid the unnecessary locking of the lock terms that are on the same page as the current lock term, due to the table construction. The overhead caused by the larger lock expenditure on row level will still have to be evaluated in practice in large-scale production environments with an extensive load.

Due to these locks, a queue will arise in the case of heavy load from interactive processing or too few COMMIT commands in batch processing. For interactive processing, this normally means that the transactions end with a time-out.

As a consequence, usability of the interactive system will be reduced to a considerable degree.

Which approaches are there to ease or, better still, to bypass the problem situation?

4.1.3   Approach

Replacing DELETE instruction by UPDATE instruction

The first measure to reduce the locks on the index should be to replace DELETE by UPDATE instructions. This is achieved by expanding the table by a status flag.

Lock Type	Lock Key	Status
Customer	4711	A
Customer	5813	D
Contract	G2603	A
Contract	YV0AA	A
Invoice	95/114	D
Voucher	1995/11/21,110341	A
...	...	...

This status flag indicates whether the lock entry is active (value A) or inactive (value D), i.e., logically deleted.

The unique key, composed of the fields `locktype` and `lock-key` should be kept without modification. The status flag is not incorporated into the index in order to avoid an index update when converting the flag to another value.

The functionality described above is changed as follows: In case of an `INSERT` instruction, the status flag is set to A, and in case of an `UPDATE` instruction that replaces the `DELETE` instruction, the status flag is set to D.

Furthermore, the response to the `SQLCODE` following the `INSERT` instruction must be modified as described below. Processing in the version without the status flag was as follows:

```
EXEC SQL
  INSERT INTO lock-table (lock-type, lock-key)
  VALUES (:hv-lock-type, :hv-lock-key)
END-EXEC
EVALUATE SQLCODE
WHEN ZERO
   everything OK, continue
WHEN -911 OR -913
   time-out, try again later
WHEN -803
   business object already locked
WHEN OTHER
   abort, system error
END-EVALUATE
```

After extension with the lock flag, the corresponding program routine would read as follows:

```
EXEC SQL
 INSERT INTO lock-table (lock-type, lock-key, status)
 VALUES (:hv-lock-type, :hv-lock-key, 'A')
END-EXEC
EVALUATE SQLCODE
WHEN ZERO
  everything OK, continue
WHEN -911 OR -913
  time-out, try again later
WHEN -803
  EXEC SQL
     UPDATE lock-table
        SET status = 'A'
     WHERE  lock-type = :hv-lock-type
     AND    lock-key = :hv-lock-key
     AND    status   = 'D'
  END-EXEC
  IF SQLCODE = 0
     everything OK, continue
  ELSE
     business object already locked
  END-IF
WHEN OTHER
  abort, system error
END-EVALUATE
```

The difference essentially consists in the modified processing of duplicate keys. On unsuccessful INSERT attempts you have now additionally to check whether an inactive lock exists. After setting such an entry to "active", actual processing can continue.

This measure reduces the activities on the index by nearly half. Important in this connection is that the status flag is not part of the index.

A further measure to solve the queuing problem consists in reducing the number of entries per table space and index page. Thus, interference with other lock entries can be minimized.

Increasing PCTFREE

To achieve this, you could enlarge the length of the lines when extending the lock key, or add a dummy field of suitable length to the table. You should however refrain from such measures since they are unpleasant from a documentation point of view. Instead you should specify a high value for the parameter

PCTFREE when defining the table space and index. In practice, the value PCTFREE 90 proved efficient for this purpose.

However, this measure takes effect only if, firstly, no table entries are deleted and, secondly, the REORG utility for the table space and index is executed with sufficient frequency. Again, the REORG utility for the index is more important. When the table grows, the value of the parameter PCTFREE can in turn be decreased successively so that there is no unnecessary wasting of disk space. This is easiest achieved by the following instructions:

```
ALTER INDEX ixname PCTFREE new-value
```

and

```
ALTER TABLESPACE tsname PCTFREE new-value
```

The REORG subsequently executed makes the registered values effective.

A third measure to reduce activities especially on the index, is to pre-load the table with a sufficient number of lines, i.e., lock terms.

Pre-load of lock table

In operational practice, the set of available values for the lock terms is often known. Customer numbers, contract numbers, invoice numbers, to list but a few examples, are often assigned according to a defined system. Therefore it is possible to generate potential lock terms, i.e., access keys, of the business objects in advance. If such a load file is loaded into the lock table prior to introducing in production, the INSERT instructions that are relatively costly compared to UPDATE instructions have to be executed only for newly generated access keys. In order to be safe from surprises, the load file should be loaded with the status flag D meaning "not active".

With this procedure, it will be reasonable to modify the INSERT routine mentioned above. Since the INSERT instruction is executed only occasionally, making the UPDATE instructions the rule, the sequence of instructions should be exchanged as follows:

```
EXEC SQL
  UPDATE lock-table
     SET status = 'A'
  WHERE lock-type = :hv-lock-type
  AND   lock-key  = :hv-lock-key
```

```
AND      status   = 'D'
END-EXEC
EVALUATE SQLCODE
WHEN ZERO
 everything ok, continue
WHEN 100
 EXEC SQL
   INSERT INTO lock-table
       (lock-type, lock-key, status)
   VALUES
       (:hv-lock-type, :hv-lock-key, 'A')
 END-EXEC
 EVALUATE SQLCODE
 WHEN ZERO
   everything ok, continue
 WHEN -803
   business object already locked
 WHEN OTHER
   abort, system error
 END-EVALUATE
WHEN -911 OR -913
 time out, try again later
WHEN OTHER
 abort, system error
END-EVALUATE
```

If it is impossible to know the future lock terms in advance, one measure is left nonetheless.

Because of the application logic, at least the lock types to be handled, the format of lock terms for the lock types and the number of lock terms to be expected per lock type should be known.

Artificial load file

With this information, you can generate a sequential load file for the lock table. By creating approximately 5 to 10 percent of the possible lock terms per lock type, you manage a fine pre-formatting of the lock table. This measure can further by optimized by specifying relatively high values for PCTFREE, for instance 80 for the table space and index. Additionally, the pre-formatted lock terms should be distributed evenly across the possible range of a lock type so that all pre-formatted pages are populated evenly. Furthermore, a particular status code can be provided for the lock terms loaded in advance - for example G meaning "generated" -- allow removal of these lock terms from the table at a later date.

We will explain this technique using a simple example. The lock type "voucher" has the access key "voucher-ID" that is structured as follows:

Position	Format	Description
1 - 4	CHAR(04)	Year, format YYYY
5 - 6	CHAR(02)	Month, format MM
7 - 8	CHAR(02)	Day, format DD
9 - 10	DECIMAL(05)	Serial number, per day

In such a case, you can create a load file containing, for every day of the year, every twentieth voucher number:

```
1996 01 01 00001
1996 01 01 00021
. . .
1996 01 01 99981
1996 01 02 00001
1996 01 02 00021

. . .
1996 12 31 00001
1996 12 31 00021

1996 12 31 99981
```

With such a load table, in this scenario, you are able to solve the essential problems on the lock table.

Summary of the measures:

• Introduction of a status flag in order to replace DELETE by UPDATE of lock terms.

• Increasing PCTFREE parameter for table space and index.

• Pre-load the table with sufficient number of suitable rows.

4.2   Avoiding Hot-Spots

4.2.1   Initial Situation

This case study describes a further infrastructure problem. This means that this functionality represents a central service for application systems.

For more and more application systems - especially in the insurance industry - there is the demand that they should support a business transaction model. This demand means that a great number of table rows in different tables can be concerned in a business-related unit of work and therefore can be changed. In the end, this business-oriented unit of work will be "committed" or "rolled back".

In this way it becomes plain that such a business-oriented unit of work has little to do with a technical unit of work. In a batch processing this corresponds to a `COMMIT` interval, i.e., the modifications that are executed between two `COMMIT` commands. In a CICS interactive process, a technical unit of work is characterized rather by the CICS instruction `SYNCPOINT`. In contrast to a technical unit of work, no time limit through technical restrictions is set for the business-related unit of work. Furthermore, it can be interrupted as often as desired.

To be able to process efficiently a unit of work in this initial situation, -- particularly interactive mode -- management functions are required to handle the changes that turn up in this unit of work. Otherwise, there would be no information as to which modified or newly added table rows belong to a specific business transaction, i.e., business-related unit of work.

A solution for this problem, workable in practice, is a central management of the business transactions. Essentially, two tables are necessary for this: a BuTra-Assign table and a BuTra-Control table (the term "BuTra" means "business transaction"). In the following, these tables are referred to as `BUTRAASGN` (BuTra-Assign table) and `BUTRACNTL` (BuTra-Control table). The basic structure of the tables is as follows:

BUTRAASGN Table:

BuTra-ID
4711
4712
5813
....

Table BUTRAASGN is used for the administration of the BuTra-IDs for each business transaction. It should be possible to generate this key automatically and in an efficient way. At the beginning of a business transaction -- copying the SQL syntax this function can be designated as OPEN BuTra -- the identifier of a business transaction is created and entered into the table. In this way, the business transaction is started.

To ensure the uniqueness of the BuTra-ID, a unique index is defined on this field.

BUTRACNTL Table:

BuTra-ID	Table	Key-Container	BuTra Status
4711	T1	12345	A
4711	T1	34567	A
4711	T2	1234567	A
4711	T3	ABC	A
...	...	...	...
5813	T1	45678	B
5813	T4	G2603	B

Table BUTRACNTL is used to enter information as to which table rows are changed by a business transaction and which status the transaction has.

The BuTra-ID serves as a connecting link between all changed information in a business transaction. It points out which table entries are changed by a business transaction.

Since a business transaction can cause changes in many different tables, information about the participating tables is necessary. It would, on principle, be sufficient to register the table name as it is determined in DB2. However, this would be a waste of space in the lock table since you would have to provide 18 bytes for this field alone. A practicable approach is the attribution of a table number to every table. If this number is defined as SMALLINT and therefore requires only 2 bytes of storage, it should be possible to code each production table of an installation. There will be relatively few installations with more than 32,768 production tables, no doubt.

In order to be able to store the structurally different access keys onto the different tables in one field, this field must not be specifically data type defined. An access key for a table can have fundamentally every permissible format and furthermore can be composed from several fields. Therefore, the key information in the lock table is defined as a character string, which requires that the key structure must be interpreted in the application.

Finally, the status of the business transaction must be stored in this table. It is required to determine whether the business transaction is still in progress (code "A") or already committed (code "B"). This basic information enables the control of a business-related unit of work.

4.2.2   Problem Description

These two tables can easily become a system bottleneck since central functions are performed on every processing in the application system, as OPEN BuTra for the initialization, UPDATE BuTra on modification, COMMIT BuTra at the successful end, and ROLLBACK BuTra for resetting a business transaction. Moreover, these functions are called very often, namely on each modification of the table rows. Which problem categories can therefore occur?

Hot-spot

Hot-spots result in the table BUTRAASGN when BuTra-Id was selected in an unsuitable way, for instance by uncritically adopting the timestamp. Accordingly, all these modifications serialize in this table.

Locking

Locking problems are connected with this topic. Since almost only modifications occur on both tables -- on table BUTRACNTL there are read accesses as well --, it is important that the locks caused by the BuTra functions mentioned above are released as rapidly as possible.

High processing load

A further demand consists in minimizing the processing load onto both tables. Because of their central position in the system, every INSERT or DELETE that is not executed enables enormous savings. The SQL commands INSERT and DELETE belong to the relatively "costly" instructions, as already mentioned.

4.2.3   Approach

Let us first consider the table BUTRAASNG. A timestamp is a good starting point to automatically ensure a uniqueness of the key BuTra-ID. However, you should not make the mistake to take it without modification as a data type for this field since otherwise precisely this table will become the bottleneck of the system.

Key distribution

By inverting the timestamp you create a key with a random distribution. An example will explain the first step:

```
Original Timestamp:  1 9 9 5 - 1 1 - 2 3 - 1 0 . 2 5 . 0 9 . 1 2 3 4 5 6

Step 1     6 5 4 3 2 1 . 9 0 . 5 2 . 0 1 - 3 2 - 1 1 - 5 9 9 1
```

This re-designed key no longer has a timestamp format. Thus, it now requires 26 bytes instead of 10. This is a waste of space that will make itself apparent especially for the table BUTRACNTL.

Optimizing the key

To improve this situation, all special characters are removed. These have no importance anyway since they are constants. Therefore, the result of the second step looks as follows:

```
Original Timestamp:  1 9 9 5 - 1 1 - 2 3 - 1 0 . 2 5 . 0 9 . 1 2 3 4 5 6

Step 1:   6 5 4 3 2 1 9 0 5 2 0 1 3 2 1 1 5 9 9 1

Step 2:   6 5 4 3 2 1 9 0 5 2 0 1 3 2 1 1 5 9 9 1
```

This results in the saving of 6 bytes. The remaining value is still too high. Since the key is numerical, it could be shortened significantly by using decimal packed format. However, this is not possible in COBOL since a maximum of 18 digits is supported in one field. By splitting the key into two fields of the same length and some re-formatting in COBOL, it is possible, however, to store this key in a character field of length 10. In a hexadecimal representation, the following figure results:

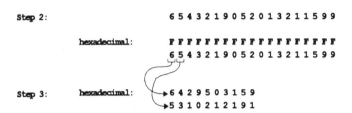

Step 2:   6 5 4 3 2 1 9 0 5 2 0 1 3 2 1 1 5 9 9

hexadecimal: F F F F F F F F F F F F F F F F F F F F
                      6 5 4 3 2 1 9 0 5 2 0 1 3 2 1 1 5 9 9

Step 3:   hexadecimal: 6 4 2 9 5 0 3 1 5 9
                          5 3 1 0 2 1 2 1 9 1

With these steps, you designed a distributed key with a length of 10 bytes based on a timestamp. Consequently, the index can be shortened significantly, in particular for table BU-TRACNTL. The risk of a hot-spot is averted virtually by the use of this key.

Another comment about BuTra-ID: Since the consecutive procurement of a timestamp can result in identical values, several INSERT attempts by the program must be planned for the table BUTRAASGN. A value of 3 attempts proved effective in practice and should be adapted, where appropriate, to the available computer configuration.

Let us now proceed to the measures in the table BUTRACNTL. The first possible and necessary measure, namely to avoid the generation of a hot-spot, was explained in connection with the table BUTRAASGN. It is achieved by constructing the distributed key BuTra-ID from a timestamp as well as by defining the clustering index, which consists of this field in the first column. Further measures are oriented to reduce the number of the "costly" operations INSERT and DELETE.

Avoiding costly operations

The first INSERT into the table BUTRACNTL occurs after calling the function OPEN BuTra. Since the key contents are already allocated through the successful INSERT into the table BU-TRAASGN, the application can delay the first INSERT into the table BUTRACNTL as long as the first modification of a row in a business-related data table occurs. In this way, with the first INSERT, the fields Table-Container and Key-Container are not inserted empty but with the corresponding contents.

Denormalization

Since data can be changed in different tables in a business transaction, there will be several rows for a particular `BuTra-ID` given the structure of the table `BUTRACNTL` as described above. For all these rows, `INSERT` functions have to be carried out. In order to be able to replace these operations by less expensive `UPDATE` operations, the table is modified in such a form that several Table-Container and Key-Container entries can be stored in one row. The following schematic table structure results:

BuTra-ID	Table-Container	Key-Container	BuTra-Status

The corresponding `CREATE` statement reads as follows:

```
CREATE TABLE butracntl
   (butra_id    CHAR(10)     NOT NULL
   ,tab_cont    CHAR(20)     NOT NULL
   ,key_cont    CHAR(400)    NOT NULL
   ,butra_st    CHAR(1)      NOT NULL)
```

In COBOL notation the fields Table-Container and Key-Container represent themselves as follows:

```
05       Table-Container      PIC X(20).
05       T-Cont-R REDEFINES Table-Container.
   10    Tab-Cont-Occ OCCURS 10.              ⇐ 10 tables
      15 Table                PIC S9(4) COMP.

05       Key-Container        PIC X(20).
05       K-Cont-R REDEFINES Key-Container.    ⇐ 10 key
                                                values
   10    Key-Cont-Occ OCCURS 10.
      15 Key                  PIC X(40).
```

Remember: Instead of the table name, a system-wide valid table number is used to save space.

The following `INSERT` operations that would result when modifying further rows in business-related data tables are replaced by more economical `UPDATE` operations. A further optimization, less effective in comparison to this one, can be achieved by adding a table counter. As a result, some search routines can be accelerated. In the example mentioned above, the different entries in the table container were limited to 10. If further entries should be necessary, a continuation line must be built up. A compromise has to be made on maximum size of the table container in order to reduce the number of continuation lines and its average occupancy level in order to optimize the disk storage requirement.

Avoiding DELETE statements

In order to further reduce the load on this table, the DELETE statement is replaced by an UPDATE statement as a supplementary measure. For the functions COMMIT BuTra and ROLLBACK BuTra, the status of the BuTra changes. While the business data are made permanent on a COMMIT BuTra, the previous modification must be removed from the database in case of a ROLLBACK BuTra. After execution of any of these functions the information on a particular BuTra in the table BU-TRACNTL is no longer required. Therefore, these rows could be deleted from the table. Instead, the field BuTra-Status can be modified in "C" meaning committed in case of a COMMIT BuTra, respectively in "D" meaning deleted.

Regular reorganization

This information about the "finished" business transactions can be removed by regular reorganization of the table.

Furthermore, the solution with updating the BuTra-Status compared to the solution with directly deleting the entry in the BU-TRACNTL table has the advantage that it enables statistical evaluations on the executed business transactions. Moreover, this information can be used for related systems.

Let us summarize the measures:

- Introduction of a distributed key based on a timestamp to avoid hot-spots.

- Denormalization of the table to reduce costly INSERT operations to the advantage of UPDATE operations.

- UPDATE of a status flag with asynchronous reorganization instead of a straight DELETE.

With the listed actions, even a "hot" table can be implemented with good performance.

4.3   Joins with Non-uniform Distribution of Attribute Values

4.3.1   Initial Situation

In this case study, we depart a bit from the infrastructure subjects that have priority of relevance for a general application design. Let us turn to a query that basically joins a table with itself.

A practical query would be: "Search for all insurance contracts in which both the risks liability and household equipment are insured". The table design represents itself as follows:

Contract No.	Risk Indicator	Attributes of Risk
42100567	Liability	...
42165381	Household equipment	...
42165381	Liability	...
94333486	Household equipment	...
94333486	Liability	...
94333486	Accident	...
...	...	...

The suitable query would read as follows:

```
SELECT ...
FROM    risktable t1
        ,risktable t2
WHERE   t1.contractnumber    = :hv-cnno
AND     t1.riskindicator = 'Liability'
--
AND     t2.contractnumber    = t1.contractnumber
AND     t2.riskindicator = 'Household equipment'
```

For contracts which contain further insured risks, this query is to be complemented correspondingly:

```
SELECT ...
FROM    risktable t1
        ,risktable t2
        ,risktable t3
WHERE   t1.contractnumber    = :hv-cnno
AND     t1.riskindicator = 'Liability'
```

```
--
   AND    t2.contractnumber    = t1.contractnumber
   AND    t2.riskindicator ='Household equipment'
--
   AND    t3.contractnumber    = t1.contractnumber
   AND    t3.riskindicator = 'Accident'
```

Normally, the Optimizer solves these queries relatively well and executes them in reasonable runtimes.

Small hit lists

This assumes relatively small hit lists for the contract number and an even distribution of the risk indicators.

Large hit lists for an ID in parallel with highly different frequencies for the restricting criteria can result in extremely different runtimes for a query.
A generalized example is given below.

```
CREATE TABLE testtab
       (id           INTEGER      NOT NULL
       ,fieldtype  SMALLINT     NOT NULL
       ,fieldvalue SMALLINT     NOT NULL
       ,further attributes)

CREATE UNIQUE INDEX itesttab ON testtab
       (id
       ,fieldtype
       ,fieldvalue)
```

In this table, there are 1,000,000 different IDs and, in total, 5 different field types. In general, the field types have the following frequencies:

Field Type	Number of Different Field Values
Type1	8000
Type2	1000
Type3	500
Type4	400
Type5	100

In the following, this query will be examined:

```
SELECT ...
 FROM   testtab t1
       ,testtab t2
```

```
        ,testtab t3
 WHERE  t1.id        = :hv-id
 AND    t1.fieldtype = :hv-fieldtype1
 --
 AND    t2.id        = t1.contractnumber
 AND    t2.fieldtype = :hv-fieldtype2
 --
 AND    t3.id        = t1.contractnumber
 AND    t3.fieldtype = :hv-fieldtype3
```

4.3.2   Problem Description

In production operation, the query shows extreme differences in runtime with the numbers and distributions mentioned above. The high runtimes are not acceptable for interactive operation.

4.3.3   Approach

First, let us consider the access path of this query. The EX-PLAIN shows the following result:

```
QUERYNO    PLANNO   METHOD
-------+--------+--------+--------+--------+-------
-+--------+-
999 1      1        0 TESTTAB  I  2  ITESTTAB N     0
NNNN   NNNN
999 1      2        1 TESTTAB  I  2  ITESTTAB N     0
NNNN   NNNN
999 1      3        1 TESTTAB  I  2  ITESTTAB N     0
NNNN   NNNN
```

Because of value distribution, the Optimizer selects the access `Matching Index Scan` with **2 MATCHCOLS** for all three steps of the query that are identified by the column `PLANNO`. The join method is nested-loop join (Method = 1). Further, the EXPLAIN results indicate that no sorting is required thanks to the suitable index.

The working method of the nested-loop join can be described as follows: First, the result set of the first query block is determined. This result set satisfied the `WHERE` condition:

```
 WHERE  t1.id        = :hv-id
  AND   t1.fieldtype = :hv-fieldtype1
```

These hits are used to enter the second query block and to form a new result set, which satisfies the following WHERE condition:

```
WHERE  t1.id        = :hv-id
AND    t1.fieldtype = :hv-fieldtype1
--
AND    t2.id        = t1.contractnumber
AND    t2.fieldtype = :hv-fieldtype2
```

The Optimizer uses this second result set to enter the third query block in order to form the final result set. This in turn will satisfy the complete WHERE condition.

Since in this case the selection of the result set is supported completely by an index, the repeated filtering of the data proceeds in such a way that the RIDs (record IDs) from the result set of the first query block are matched to the hits of the second query block, and these in turn are matched to the hits of the third query block.

Let us play this procedure through for several cases:

Case	Number of RIDs in 1st Query Block	Number of RIDs in 2nd Query Block	Number of RIDs in 3rd Query Block
1	10000	1000	10
2	1000	10000	10
3	10	1000	10000

In case 1, the 10,000 RIDs from the first query block are matched to the 1,000 RIDs from the second query block. That means checking for each of the 10,000 RIDs whether it satisfies the condition of the second query block. Processing continues with the resulting list of RIDs. For each of these RIDs -- their number being between 0 and 1,000 --, it is checked in turn, whether it satisfies the condition of the third query block. The resulting hit list contains 0 to 10 hits. The reduction of the hit lists takes place only at the end of processing.

Sequence of query blocks in the case of joins

Processing already looks a bit more favorable in case 2. For the 1,000 RIDs, it is checked whether they satisfy the condition of the second query block. The resulting RID list contains 0 to 1,000 entries. For each entry of this list, it is checked whether it satisfies the condition of the third query block. In this way, the final hit list of the complete query is reduced to 0 to 10 hits as in the first case. But as compared to the first case, insofar less internal processing occurs as less RIDs have to be matched to the hit list from the second query block.

Finally, let us consider the third case. The RID list of the fist query block contains 10 entries. For each of these entries it is checked whether it satisfies the condition of the second query block. The resulting RID list contains 0 to 10 entries. This RID list is matched to the third query block in order to determine the final hit list. Fewer tests are executed internally, since in this case operation takes place on very small RID lists.

The strategy for optimal runtimes of such queries therefore exists in processing the smallest hit list first and to use the resulting RID list to check against the next query block.

How to convert this strategy in an application?

Dynamic SQL

When using dynamic SQL, DB2 automatically pursues this strategy since the Optimizer knows the values of the host variables when dynamically binding the query. Provided that corresponding catalog values are available from a RUNSTATS utility, the Optimizer will decide on the most cost-effective access path. This access path would correspond to case 3.

In certain cases, this course of action can be taken into account for a batch application. In an on-line application, however, dynamic SQL has usually no place at all, since the ratio between the times for dynamic binding and executing the SQL statement is too poor. In contrast to a batch execution profile which is characterized rather by a rare execution of statements with large hit lists, an on-line application profile is characterized by SQL statements that are executed often, but process small hit lists. This also applies to cursors having large hit lists. Since within a CICS environment the clause WITH HOLD is not permitted for cursors, the cursor is closed after the next SYNC-POINT being caused by transmitting the screen. Therefore, a cursor in an on-line environment also has a small hit list. After paging the screen, dynamic binding would have to be repeated.

Therefore, let us consider the normal case, namely static SQL. Here, the access path is determined when binding the package. Since one usually works with host variables, the Optimizer can not take into account the values of the host variables that are known only at the package's runtime.

This means that there is normally no possibility to affect the access path with static SQL. This should also be avoided for reasons of the application's maintainability.

Stable distribution
of values

An exception should at most be taken into account with extreme non-uniform distributions of attributes. Knowledge about this distribution may be integrated into the application by assigning values to the host variables depending on the contents. In this scenario there is a risk that the distribution of the attributes in the database changes over the time without the program structures being adapted to the changed situation.

4.4 Formulation of Restart Keys in Cursors

4.4.1 Initial Situation

This case study considers one of the normal cases of an application more closely, namely a cursor with a restart clause.

We are working in a table `testtab` with the clustering index `itesttab` that consists of the columns `col1`, `col2`, and `col3`.

The cursor is defined as follows:

```
SELECT    col1, col2, col3,...
  FROM      testtab
  ORDER BY col1
          ,col2
          ,col3
```

However, this definition alone which only provides for a correct hit list, is of little use for an application. Due to COMMIT points, the cursor is closed again and again. This applies in particular to CICS environments where this is already caused by the transmission of a screen. Consequently, the cursor requires restart logic. This will change its appearance as follows:

```
SELECT    col1
         ,col2
         ,col3
         ,further fields,...
FROM      testtab
WHERE     col1 > :hv-col1
OR        col1 = :hv-col1 AND col2 > :hv-col2
OR        col1 = :hv-col1 AND col2 = :hv-col2
                           AND col3 > :hv-col3
ORDER BY col1, col2, col3
```

The fields `hv-col1`, `hv-col2`, and `hv-col3` represent the corresponding host variables.

By storing the fetched row, the application is able to restart after closure of the cursor. Consequently, the next row that is not yet read, is provided with the first FETCH of the cursor after re-opening.

Alternatively, the restart logic could be achieved by concatenating the fields of the restart key. This would read as follows:

```
SELECT    col1
          ,col2
          ,col3
          ,further fields,...
FROM      testtab
WHERE     col1 || col2 || col3 > :hv-restartkey
ORDER BY col1, col2, col3
```

No concatenation of composed keys

The resulting set for this formulation is the same as for the one described first. At runtime, however, no index is used with the second formulation even if it is suitably built up. Therefore, this solution is out of question both in batch as in on-line operations. Independent of this negative effect and for reasons of standardization, one should strive fundamentally that a function -- here restart conditions -- is always realized in the same way.

After having described the fundamental restart logic for a cursor whose restart key consists of multiple columns, we now come to the actual problem.

In a normal application, the data for an access key must be provided with a cursor in a given sort. For further consideration, the restart key should consist of two columns and the supporting index should be composed of the columns (id, col1, col2). Hence, the cursor structure is as follows:

```
SELECT    col1
          ,col2
          ,col3
          ,further fields,...
FROM      testtab
WHERE     id   = :hv-id
AND (     col1 > :hv-col1
OR        col1 = :hv-col1 AND col2 > :hv-col2
    )
ORDER BY col1
          ,col2
```

Note that the field id surely does not appear in the SELECT list: it is already known on account of the WHERE condition after all.

4.4.2   Problem Description

With the given functionally correct formulation of the cursor, you will find with an EXPLAIN that the Optimizer selects the access path with the index mentioned. The indicator MATCHCOLS has value 1, namely the id.

In this case, the Optimizer does not recognize the obvious, also delivered by the restart clauses: col1 >= :hv-col1. Using this information, the indication MATCHCOLS could be increased by 1.

The effect should be clear actually. With a large hit list for the clause WHERE id = :hv-id, DB2 has to process significantly more RIDs internally as when processing two matching index columns.

4.4.3   Approach

By incorporating the supplementary, in fact redundant formulation with the operator >=, the access path is optimized by a further matching column:

```
SELECT    col1
          ,col2
          ,further fields,...
FROM      testtab
WHERE     id   =  :hv-id
AND       col1 >= :hv-col1
AND (     col1 >  :hv-col1
OR        col1 =  :hv-col1 AND col2 > :hv-col2)
ORDER BY col1, col2
```

The EXPLAIN of this query points out that the use of index columns in the access path, a Matching Index Scan, is improved from one column to two columns.

4.5   Reducing Synchronous IOs for Hierarchical Structures

4.5.1   Initial Situation

The number of synchronous IOs is one of the most important influence factors on the response time of a data access, as we have seen repeatedly. Emphasis is on the term "synchronous". This means that the data to be provided is not available in a cache of a data medium or in one of the DB2 buffer pools or DB2 hiper pools - which basically represent a cache as well - but have to be read directly from disk. Therefore, the greater part of the total response time consists of disk response time.

	Central Storage DB2 Buffer Pool	Expanded Storage DB2 Hiper Pool	Cache Controller IBM 3390	DASD IBM 3390 Model 1. 2. 3
Provisioning	0 ms	0.04 ms	0.98 ms	17.6 ms
Time	0 s	1 s	24.5 s	M1 = 7.33 min M2 = 8.58 min M3 = 9.62 min

The table compares the provisioning times for one page.

If the page is in the buffer pool, it is immediately provided. For transferring one page from a hiper pool, i.e., from the Expanded Storage you have to reckon 40 microseconds. But provisioning from a cache controller requires already 980 microseconds. The IBM 3390 Model 1, the fastest model of this series, manages the transfer of one page in 17.6 microseconds.

In order to clarify the order of magnitude, the provisioning time from the Expanded Storage is standardized to 1 second in the last line of the table. Then, 24.5 seconds are required from the cache controller, and already 7 to almost 10 minutes directly from disk. Provisioning of one page directly from disk corresponds to the term "synchronous IO".

In the same time, business-transaction-oriented applications become more and more important, as described already in a former case study. Three essential components are detectable with these systems: The first component is processing of business objects instead of single rows, the second one is the size, i.e., the unit of work of a business transaction, and the third one is the internal structure of the business objects.

A business object is characterized, from a database point of view, by the fact that we no longer deal with one row in one table but instead we may have to deal with several rows, which are stored in one or more tables.

A business transaction can be considered as its generalization, once again from a database point of view. The business-related unit of work, a synonym for a business transaction, consists of the processing, i.e., the modifying of one or more business objects.

Therefore, a prerequisite for processing a business transaction is first the retrieval of the affected business objects.

Let us come to the interior structure of the business objects. For reasons of flexibility many modern systems are designed with as few built-in hierarchies as possible. A characteristic example is IAA (Insurance Application Architecture). IAA is a collection of rule sets for insurance applications. It comprises methodical principles and contents for data, function, and process modeling. Since 1990, IAA is being developed by IBM in cooperation with leading insurance companies.

This is not the place to enter the business-related topics. Instead, we will work out with which design principles from a data modeling point of view the desired flexibility is to be achieved, and which effects result in the database design.

The basic characteristics of the data model can be described as follows:

- All keys have the same data format.
- All keys have a uniform distribution.
- All relations are mapped exclusively via relation entities.

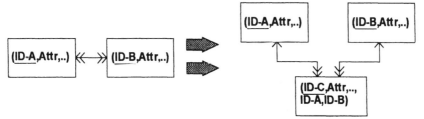

Avoidance of hot-spots, small reorganization need

By assigning uniform keys on principle, it is possible to provide a unique format. The distributed assignment has the advantage, as we have already noticed, that it firstly avoids hot-spots and secondly reduces the reorganization need of a table. The design decision in favor of distributed keys in a table quite considers performance aspects which in particular show very positive effects in the case of INSERT.

From the above design principles, one fact is not very obvious but should be mentioned explicitly. Due to this key construction, keys composed of several fields are not provided and therefore not possible.

Let us consider the conversion of relations somewhat closer. A business object can consist of many rows in one or more tables.

One of the known 1:n foreign key relations between two independent business objects, e.g., between customer and contract, is converted as follows:

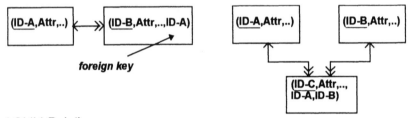

Parent-Child-Relation

The parent-child-relation is the other known 1:n foreign key relation. An example from the insurance industry is the relation between a damage and the associated payments, another one from trade the relation between order and order item. This relation can be illustrated graphically in the following form:

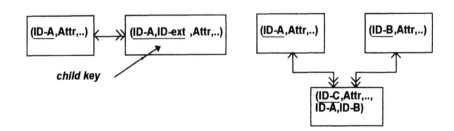

This relation, too, is implemented in a relation entity for reasons of uniformity and flexibility.

Remarkable with the solution with distributed keys, but consistently solved, is that for a parent-child-relation the associated parent key can not be derived from the key-value of the child.

The same design guidelines apply to the relation entities. The key of a relation entity is independent; only via the foreign keys is it detectable which entities are related with each other.

The category of a n:m relation is represented, on principle, only with a relation entity. The above-mentioned applies in this case, too: The key of the relation entity is independent.

4.5.2 Problem Description

As already mentioned above, the design guideline to exclusively use uniform distributed, uniquely formatted keys has in certain areas quite positive effects on the performance. Essentially, the avoidance of hot-spots and the reduction of reorganization needs are to be listed. However, by complying consistently with these principles, you also bargain for certain problems. Predominantly, the following problems can be recognized:

- increased number of tables,
- increased number of table rows,
- increased number of indexes.

These problem areas will be explained in detail.

Using relation entities

The increased number of tables is caused primarily by implementing relation entities for 1:n relations as well. Traditionally, these relations would be implemented by a foreign key, as shown in the figure above, without requiring a separate table for the relation entity.

From a business-oriented point of view it has to be considered at least for the "genuine" relations between independent business objects whether the flexibility obtained by the relation entity is required at all. For most parent-child-relations, however, this flexibility will hardly be necessary.

The use of relation entities for 1:n relations also involves more table rows being managed compared to the traditional method with foreign keys, namely the rows in the relation entity.

More indexes

If the keys of the dependent object of a parent-child-relation are independent from the key of the parent object, two indexes are required to ensure uniqueness: a unique index on the key of the child table and, additionally, an index on the foreign key, namely the key of the parent table. For this construction, however, this key is not available in the child table but evacuated into the relation entity. This necessitates, firstly, an index to ensure uniqueness in the relation table, and a further one, being composed of the keys of the parent and child tables. With a classical construction of a child key, for instance being composed of the parent key and a serial number, only one index is required for the child table to meet both requirements -- uniqueness and access through the parent key.

The points just mentioned are relatively easy to recognize from outside since they can be derived through indicative figures from the DB2 catalog. They are closely connected with the administration expenditures involved with a system.

Besides these external symptoms, the following internal problem areas become manifest:

- increased disk storage requirement,
- increased number of synchronous IOs for SELECT,
- increased expenditure for INSERT and DELETE,
- costly usage of joins.

As already suggested above, more key fields are managed as compared to traditional database modeling when consistently using one-column, distributed keys. This is recognizable especially when using relation entities for 1:n relations: disk storage requirement is increased both for tables as for indexes. However, this effect is of somewhat subordinate importance compared to the following, runtime-related arguments.

Costly accesses on child objects

Due to the consistent distribution of the keys on the dependent levels of a business object as well, the entries to one parent key are distributed over the entire table. A short explanation: The child key that is assigned independently from the parent key, must be defined as an index with the key words UNIQUE and CLUSTER. The uniqueness should be plain; the property CLUSTER is required to ensure that this key is actually distributed to avoid a hot-spot. As a result, the clause CLUSTER is no longer available for the index that supports the access via the parent key. Therefore, to read the child data for a given parent, in the extreme case, a GETPAGE request must be issued for each child. It is obviously less expensive if the child data for a given parent were clustered according to the parent key and were thus situated in very few -- often even only one or two -- pages.

The increased number of indexes in the case of child tables, justified above, raises the price of the INSERT and DELETE operations. Instead of one index for ensuring the functions "uniqueness" and "access via parent key" in the case of classical modeling, in the flexible variant there are always two indexes to manage. This effect is especially drastic if the index that supports access via the parent key has long RID chains. This is the case when this index only consists of the parent key and, for example, the child table is the order item table with many order items to one order.

If a business object consists of several 1:n relations, the solution with the flexible, one-column, distributed keys forces a read of the entire business object, even if only a dependent part is required. The access key of the business object is usually available as a key only on the top level and the directly subordinated level. If the hierarchy of a business object is further developed, the chaining of the foreign keys must always be read as well via the relation entities. This normally happens by using SQL joins, since "hand-written" joins are mostly even slower.

To conclude the problem description, we will schematically present the IO behavior of a business object that consists of three hierarchy levels and has 10 child entries for each entry. We further suppose a record length of prevalent 250 bytes and that the business object itself is not yet located in a buffer pool, hiper pool, or cache. The size of the buffer pools is such that the root and all intermediate pages of the indexes are located in the buffer pools.

With a traditional solution, the IO behavior presents itself as follows:

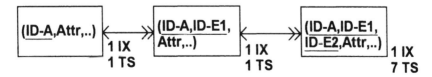

ID-A designates the parent key. ID-E1 designates the key extension of the second hierarchy level which forms, together with the key extension of ID-A, a unique key. ID-E2 designates the key extension of the third hierarchy level. This in turn forms, together with ID-A and ID-E1, a unique key. The index which for our purposes is the only index on each level, is built of these key columns. This index is UNIQUE <u>and</u> CLUSTER.

To read the top hierarchy level, one synchronous IO is required for the leaf page of the index and another one for reading the data page with the corresponding row. Since the index of the second hierarchy level is clustered according to the parent key ID-A, all index entries to the parent key in turn will usually be located on one index page. Correspondingly, there is also one synchronous IO on the index page. Since the index is clustered according to the parent key, the child data to this parent key is also located on one page. Consequently, all data on the second hierarchy level can be provided with only one GETPAGE request, i.e., one synchronous IO. According to the prerequisites mentioned above, 100 rows are to be read on the third hierarchy level. Since they are clustered according to the parent key as well, you can also start from the fact that only one leaf page of the index and 7 pages of the table have to be read. In total, the entire business object is provided by the execution of 12 synchronous IOs. With a disk response time of 25 milliseconds, this processing requires 0.3 seconds in total.

When opposing this implementation of a business object with the consistent and complete conversion using a one-column and distributed key, the following results:

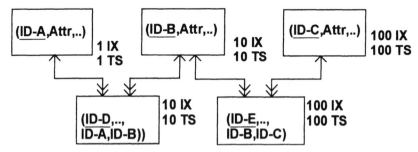

The fields ID-A, ID-B, and ID-C are the unique keys of the first, second, and third hierarchy level that are independent from each other. No relation between them is recognizable. ID-D and ID-E are the unique keys of the relation entities between the first and second and, respectively, second and third hierarchy levels. The keys of the first and second and, respectively, second and third hierarchy levels are stored as foreign keys in these relation entities. To read the first hierarchy level, one synchronous IO is required on the leaf page of the index and another one on a data page. To be able to read the second hierarchy level, the relation entity between the first and the second hierarchy level must be read. The query on this relation entity has the form:

```
SELECT  id-b
FROM    relation-entity-d
WHERE   id-a = :hv-id-a
```

Since it is not clustered according to the parent key, 10 GET-PAGE requests are required on the index leaf pages, which contain the RIDs for the WHERE condition, and on the associated data pages. In this way, the ten different values of ID-B are known. The second hierarchy level is clustered according to ID-B, thus the values that have just been determined are located in different pages. This applies both to the index leaf pages and to the data pages. For each row of the middle hierarchy level for this business object there are ten dependent rows in the third hierarchy level. The keys to these 100 rows can be determined, as already described, only by retrieving the relation entities between the second and third hierarchy level. For the relation entities, as in the previous description, 100 GETPAGE requests are executed for the index leaf pages and for the data pages. The same numbers apply to the third hierarchy level. Summing up the GETPAGE requests results in 442 synchronous IOs. The resulting total response time of approximately 11 seconds would not be acceptable for an on-line operation.

In contrast to the first implementation that was designed with key extensions, the response times of this conversion are increased by the factor - not the percentage - 37. This example makes clear which possible additional costs are caused by stubbornly implemented flexibility.

While maintaining the flexibility of the second solution, this ratio can be improved essentially by providing the index leaf pages and the data pages as well in the buffer pools and hiper pools. However, extensions of the main memory or of the extended memory belong to the most expensive measures when upgrading a machine in order to gain performance.

Let us consider approaches that maintain a suitable flexibility at reasonable costs.

4.5.3   Approach

It was already mentioned at the beginning of this case study that distributed keys have positive effects on the system performance. For this reason, a well-balanced usage of this key construction should be retained.

In the following, pragmatic approaches are presented for three business scenarios:

- n:m relation between business objects

- 1:n relation between business objects

- 1:n relation within a business object

Relation entities for n:m relations

The only way to realize a n:m relation between business objects is the use of a relation entity. In the borderline case when a 1:n relation is expected to become a n:m relation shortly, for reasons of flexibility this solution should be adopted as well.

Foreign key for 1:n relations

For performance reasons, it is recommended to implement a 1:n relation between business objects with the aid of a foreign key attribute on the object's "n-side". An index is defined on this attribute to support read operations. The UNIQUE and CLUSTER index is already reserved for the primary key of the n-object.

In case there are several 1:n relations between two business objects, several foreign key attributes should be provided in the n-object. The following 1:n relations between the business objects partner and insurance contract are examples for this case: partner as contract partner (C), partner as insured person (IP), partner as recipient of payment (RP). The tables can be schematically represented as follows, reduced to the fields being of relevance in this context:

```
partner(pt-no, partner-attributes)
contract(cn-no, contract-attributes, pt-c, pt-ip ,pt-rp)
```

Finally let us consider the 1:n relation within a business object. In this scenario, it is recommended that the primary key of the business object is assigned in a distributed way. This is the key of the top hierarchy level. For the further, hierarchy dependent levels, the means of key extension should be used. This construction saves one index on every dependent level, and furthermore enables to use the composed key thus formed as UNIQUE and CLUSTER index. The advantages when reading the entire business object are obvious. Beyond the described advantages, the key inheritance opens up the possibility to read every level independently from the superordinate ones, since the primary key of the business object is known on every level. Key distribution at the top level of the business object involves implicitly the same distribution at the subordinate levels as well so that there is no risk of hot-spots either.

Distributed key on top level

The characteristics of this solution can be summarized as follows:

- Reduced REORG requirements by distributing the first index column of the clustering index on all hierarchy levels.

- Owing to the clustering index, read operations on subordinate levels cause fewer GETPAGE requests.

- Owing to the reduction of the index number, INSERT and DELETE operations become less expensive.

4.6   Comparison of LOAD and INSERT Procedures

4.6.1   Initial Situation

When designing extensive processing with high modification rates, you are often forced to balance performance arguments against architectural arguments.

In this case study, the arguments for load and INSERT procedures are compared. Further, some approaches for load procedures are pointed out.

Using a transaction-oriented processing procedure with IN-SERT, UPDATE, and DELETE commands is justified, on the one hand, by a more consistent design of the application, on the other hand by ensuring improved parallelism.

Let us consider some aspects of the INSERT/UPDATE procedure.

Consistency between on-line and batch processing

Often, specific functionality is required both in on-line operation for processing small amounts as well as in batch for bulk processing. In this case, it is advantageous in the development phase of an application to design and implement this functionality only once. The expenditure for design and implementation is minimized and you can concentrate on one implementation. Compared to separated procedures for on-line and batch processing, programming is significantly facilitated.

This procedure offers advantages for the subsequent operation in production, too. During later modifications, enhancements, and error corrections as well, changes are required only in one place. As a result, the consistency of the application and therefore the future error rate is affected positively.

Because of the identical processing sequence for a unit of work, on-line and batch processing are automatically compatible with each other. This means that the probability for deadlocks is very small when on-line and batch processing take place in parallel. Queues occur at most when the load is sufficiently high.

A processing logic, however, which is adjusted to process small amounts does not necessarily represent the most economical variant for batch processing. A great number of INSERT, UP-DATE, and DELETE instructions in a batch processing will cause significant overhead by the intensive use of the log data set. This situation becomes even more critical if too few COM-MIT instructions are issued. Then, the ROLLBACK time can be considerable.

Prefetch with on-line and batch

Because of the procedure being optimized for small numbers of SQL statements, performance factors like sequential prefetch are scarcely used. In an on-line processing, this would even be contra-productive since using such functions causes too much overhead. On the contrary, in on-line functions you usually switch off this property by using the clause OPTIMIZE FOR 1 ROW. For batch operation, however, this measure has completely negative effects on the elapsed time.

In order to be able to guarantee recovery times as short as possible in the case of a later crash, a FULLCOPY is appropriate after a mass INSERT/UPDATE/DELETE. Furthermore, a REORG can also be sensible in order to positively affect the state of the table with regard to performance. In this context, the indicator CLUSTERRATIO shall be mentioned.

Let us come to the analysis of a load procedure.

Arguments for a load procedure

The safety of this procedure is to be classified as equally good as compared to an INSERT/UPDATE/DELETE procedure. The prerequisite for this safety level is a comparably intensive test. Since such a procedure is used in production under the control of a job scheduling system, the response to errors is as secure as for the other procedure.

Compared to the INSERT procedure, in most cases shorter runtimes are achieved since a load procedure is used only from a certain order of magnitude onwards. The supplementary time required for unloading and loading the table and the time savings gained by replacing the SQL instructions by sequential data processing, must be balanced with the time for the direct SQL instructions. In most cases, this will favor the load procedure from an order of magnitude of more than 10 percent of data to be modified.

Option LOG NO

When using the load utility with the option LOG NO, logging of the changes to the data base is turned off. This saves overhead, but necessitates a subsequent FULL COPY. However, such a procedure is more favorable with regard to runtimes as the use of the option LOG YES, which does not urgently require subsequent back up. Furthermore, in case of a problem, a serviceable state of the data base is restored faster with the FULL COPY.

When using the load procedure, the unloaded data is sorted with the sequential output of the application before being reloaded into the table. By this step, the table is implicitly reorganized to the benefit of the on-line operation.

Higher test
expenditure with
load procedure

The higher complexity is a disadvantage of the load procedure. Instead of the "natural" SQL statements INSERT, UPDATE, and DELETE in the application program, supplementary jobs with DB utilities and the corresponding control statements must be supplied. The expenditure for testing the correct processing of these jobs is significantly higher for the load procedure than for the other procedure.

Load procedure
prevents
concurrency

Compared to the procedure with embedded SQL statements, the table is locked for all other accesses while the load job is running, and for all write accesses while the backup is running. For this, it is assumed that COMMIT points are issued sufficiently often in the case of the procedure with SQL statements. Otherwise, a solid hindrance to other requests occurs here as well. In this way, you are once again in the situation to balance the wider locking by the load procedure against the long elapsed times of the other procedure. You cannot get the advantages of the shorter runtimes for nothing.

4.6.2   Problem Description

The potential problems which can occur due to using procedures designed for online for bulk updates in batch, are summarized briefly:

- The online procedure mostly requires too long elapsed time.

- Sometimes, a utilization of the log data set that is too high arises through the dialog procedure.

- The time to restore a table can be too long for production operation.

4.6.3   Approach

First, a solution is presented which manages long runtimes without using a load utility.

The approach consists in running several jobs with the same application program in parallel. The SQL instructions INSERT, UPDATE, and DELETE are maintained in the program without modification.

Paralleling of a batch program

This approach presupposes the avoidance of locking conflicts between the batch jobs. This is supported best if the tables to be modified are partitioned and if each of the jobs processes exactly one partition. This presupposes that the input data for the batch jobs has been split by a preceding job according to the partitioning of the tables that are to be modified. Thus it is ensured that the programs running in parallel can no longer cross their paths on the clustering index since only this index can be partitioned.

Deadlocks on secondary indexes

For the other indexes, however, deadlocks must be expected. Several approaches are conceivable for this situation.

Duplicated table without secondary indexes

If only INSERT operations are executed on the output table, there is the possibility to create a permanent copy of this table. This copy has the same clustering index as the original table, but no further indexes. Before starting the paralleled programs, this table duplicate is cleared. The application program is modified inasmuch as it is performing its INSERTs on this copy and no longer to the original table. On completion of all parallel jobs, the contents of this table is inserted into the original. This can be done, for example, with a SPUFI batch job with the following control statements:

```
INSERT INTO original
SELECT * FROM copy
;
```

Since the copy has the same structure as the original table, this solution is feasible without using a utility.

Deleting and re-building the secondary indexes

A more complex alternative for the procedure with the duplicated table consists in first building the control statements for a REBIND of the packages from the DB2 catalog which include access paths using the secondary indexes of the table. In the next step, the secondary indexes of the table are dropped. After this action, the parallel jobs are executed. Obviously, the SQL statements affect the original table when using this variant. The jobs can no longer interfere with each other on the secondary indexes of the table. On the clustering index, they cannot anyhow because of the separation of the input data. On completion of all parallel jobs the secondary indexes are re-built, best with the option DEFER. This option causes only the entry into the DB2 catalog, not the actual index setup. For performance reasons, this is done with the utility RECOVER INDEX. Finally, the control statements built up at the beginning for the

REBIND of the packages are executed. For security reasons, a FULL COPY is advisable here just as it was for the other procedure.

Paralleling the application programs has the positive effect that the total time required can be reduced clearly without blocking the table by the LOAD utility as in the case of the pure load procedure.

Components of a load procedure

Now the second approach will be considered. It represents the pure case of a load procedure. This procedure is characterized by the fact that the following steps must be executed:

1. Unloading the tables to be modified by INSERT, UPDATE, or DELETE operations.

2. Running the application program. The INSERT and UPDATE operations onto the tables are replaced by WRITE instructions on one sequential output file per modified table. The DELETE instructions remain unchanged.

3. Sorting the output files with the associated load files.

4. Reloading the output files of the SORT steps into the corresponding tables.

5. Backup

6. RUNSTATS utility

7. REBIND utility

The following comments apply to this procedure:

- An application program without DELETE operations can run in parallel with the unload utilities. If, for example, the tables hold temporary data it can be assumed that no deletions occur.

- If the application program includes DELETE operations the unload jobs can only be run after the application program in which the INSERT and UPDATE instructions have been replaced by WRITE instructions. For better restartability of the entire batch procedure, a FULL COPY is advisable before running the batch program. If the entire procedure needs to be restarted, "only" a RECOVER utility needs to run.

Replacing DELETE statements by UPDATE statements

For better paralleling of the procedure it is worthwhile to consider replacing the DELETE operations by UPDATE operations. Deletion of a row is then replaced by updating a delete flag that has been added to the table. In this way, the corresponding table can be unloaded in parallel to the execution of the application program, thus the total time of the procedure can be reduced.

Now, let us come in for sorting. Schematically, the sort step has the following structure:

```
//SORT        EXEC SORT
//SORTIN       DD  DISP=SHR,DSN=batch-output
//             DD  DISP=SHR,DSN=unload-data
//SORTOUT      DD  DISP=OLD,DSN=load-data
//SYSIN        DD  *
  SORT FIELDS=(.....),EQUALS
  SUM FIELDS=NONE
```

Option EQUALS

The SORT FIELDS instruction includes the UNIQUE index of the table. Owing to the option EQUALS, duplicate keys with regard to the SORT FIELDS parameter are kept in the input order. For non-unique keys, the SUM FIELDS instruction removes all records but the first one.

If additionally the DELETE statements are replaced by WRITE instructions as described above, the sort step must be completed by the additional option OMIT:

```
OMIT COND=(p1,m1,f1,EQ,'D')
```

Hereby, p1 stands for the start position, m1 for the length, and f1 for the format of the delete flag in the record. The delete flag will probably have the format CHAR(1). This instruction prevents logically deleted records that are recognizable by the value "D" in the delete flag from being transferred into the output data set of the sort step.

The subsequent load utility is started with the options REPLACE and LOG NO for speed optimization. Therefore, a backup must be executed. A FULL COPY recommends itself.

In the case of high modifications rates, it can be appropriate to run the RUNSTATS utility and the REBIND of the involved packages after the FULL COPY. The catalog values may possibly be greatly changed by the RUNSTATS so access paths must be observed carefully.

The basic load procedure is hereby described.

Beyond the steps described here, the following modifications of this procedure are to be encountered commonly.

Combination of
load procedure
and paralleling

Firstly, it is possible to combine the load procedure with the parallelization of the batch program described previously. This presupposes a partitioned table, so that batch jobs can be executed without mutual hindrance. Often, the total time can be reduced by this measure. A further refinement of this procedure consists of splitting the unload jobs and sorting in several jobs which process only one partition each. However, this presupposes advanced programming techniques that are described in the following.

Restriction to one partition

In specific cases, it can happen that a batch job only changes one partition in one run. One example for such an application is the invoicing runs for the individual months against a table that is clustered according to the months. In this case, it is completely sufficient to unload and later to re-load only the affected partition.

In practice, however, the difficulty is to automate such a procedure. If, for each run, the job scheduling staff has to manually enter the modifications of the control statements for the utilities into the job control system, this is a risky and error-prone implementation.

Generation of the control statement by the application program

In practice, it proved effective that the application program uses its input data to generate the control statements and to write them on sequential files. These files are used as control files for the utility jobs. In order to do so, the batch program has to create the following statements:

- SELECT instruction to unload one partition
- Load instruction to load one partition of the table

```
LOAD DATA LOG NO INTO table PART n REPLACE
```

- COPY instruction to save the partition of the table space

```
COPY tablespace DSNUM n FULL YES
```

By the fact that the application program generates the control statement for the unload job, this job can run only after the application program. Once again, the gain of time through unloading only one partition has to be weighed against the advantage of paralleling in the case of the other procedure. Only for very large tables with many partitions this procedure will pay off. To give an example: Such a procedure was applied to a table with a target size of 80 million rows and 16 partitions.

The remaining steps of the selective procedure correspond to those of the complete load procedure.

5 Tuning

5.1 Unavoidable Tuning Measures

The preceding chapters described numerous measures to develop DB2 application systems in such a way that they should cause relatively few performance problems.

Nonetheless, the necessity to carry out tuning measures at short notice will arise again and again. Two such common situations are discussed briefly in this section. The first one is a new release of the database and the other one is a change in user approach.

Tuning because of a new release

With a new release of the database, it has been repeatedly seen that the Optimizer, which selects the access paths undergoes massive changes -- generally, it is improved. This can render tuning measures that were set up for the previous version of the Optimizer obsolete and, in individual cases, even adversely affect the performance. In such cases, it is particularly important that the tuning measures be documented well and in an easily accessible manner.

Change in user behavior

Now to the users' behavior. As pointed out earlier, performance measures are advisable and can cause positive effects only if the importance or frequency of accesses has been included in the design considerations. When these parameters change, those accesses that will become important or critical from then on should be tuned.

5.2   Economical Procedure with ABC Analysis

In situations with performance problems, high pressure is applied to the involved departments -- Application Development and Systems Engineering -- to solve the problems that have come up. On the one hand, from the users' point of view, the problem has to be solved in a very short time -- else they would not be able to carry on their work in a cost-effective manner which is a necessity. On the other hand, the solution of the problem must be reasonably priced as well. Both requirements call for an economical procedure.

Such a standard procedure, well known in applied economics, is the ABC analysis or 80:20 rule. This principle postulates that 80% of the resources are required by just 20% of the consumers.

System load is concentrated on few transactions

Applied to our situation, this means that very few transactions consume a large part of the resources. By tuning precisely those transactions, it is possible to achieve the highest obtainable effect with the lowest effort.

The procedure described below deals with the identification of these large resource consumers as fast as possible, and subjecting them to tuning.

The basic conditions for this procedure that was developed in a tuning project and refined in further, subsequent projects are as follows in an on-line production environment:

- MVS

- DB2

- CICS

- For small groups of programs, i.e., generally, fewer than 10 programs, one transaction code each was assigned in CICS.

5.3   Sequence of the Activities

5.3.1   First Step: Providing Information

The following information per transaction code is determined from statistical systems such as the CICS Manager or the MICS:

- number of program calls per day,
- total CPU time (incl. DB2 time),
- CPU time per transaction,
- worst transactions per day.

This data is collected for about 10 days. Since this information is usually available in generation data sets, its creation causes no delay in the procedures. There is the positive effect, however, of eliminating outliers.

Two hit-lists are formed with this information:

- one according to the sum of the CPU time,
- one by worst transaction.

However, the more important hit-list is the one according to CPU time, since the second evaluation includes information about outliers, despite the creation of the time-series.

Tuning procedures only for a few transactions

The tuning measures should concentrate on the five to ten largest consumers of resources. Tuning a transaction that consumes 20,000 CPU seconds daily by 10% saves 2,000 CPU seconds. The value of this effort is certainly greater than the value of tuning a transaction that consumes 1000 CPU seconds daily, with a tuning factor of 50%.

5.3.2   Second Step: Creating Access Profiles

The first activity identified the tuning candidates. No judgment is made about whether the transactions found are "good" or "bad", because the criterion for their quality has not been considered so far. In most cases, it does not even exist, but has to be determined for the subsequent steps to be taken.

Access profile

Such a practicable scale would be the access profile, which has been introduced in the previous chapters. The access profile documents the ideas of the developer as to how a transaction should access the data, i.e., which access paths the Optimizer should select for the SQL statements, using the indexes.

5.3.3   Third Step: Analysis of Access Profile and Explain

By comparing the statements of the access profile with the Explain of the package you will obtain, in practically all cases, the starting point for the further tuning activities. Transactions whose actual access paths conform to the Explain will be considered later, since they work exactly the way they have been originally designed by the developer. For the other transactions, it has to be checked why, from the DB2 point of view, they are working differently from what was planned.

5.3.4   Fourth Step: Analysis of the Tuning Candidates

After the tuning candidates have been selected in the first three steps, the actual examination can start. Considering the effort required, the sequence of the tuning measures to be taken for these transactions is as follows:

Examining the SQL statements

If the desired access profile and Explain, i.e., the actual access path, do not correspond, the "simplest" causes can often be found in the formulation of the SQL statement. With a -- from the Optimizer's point of view -- "more favorable" combination of the WHERE conditions such as the replacement of OR linkages by the BETWEEN or IN clause, an attempt must be made to achieve the planned access path. Detailed information as to which statements should be avoided can be found, in particular, in the Administration Guide. There, the WHERE conditions are classified according to how much resources they require, i.e., to what extent index usage is possible at all. However, one must be careful when making categorical statements such as "OR linkages are basically bad". The resolution of the SQL statements depends on the Optimizer release and version. Hence, an orientation to the currently used release is imperative. Therefore, this is not the place to make complete statements about the definition of the access paths for all times.

Notes on SQL formulation in the Administration Guide

Nonetheless, some examples of costly commands that were encountered repeatedly are being consideredbelow.

Often, too many columns are qualified in the SELECT list or in the UPDATE command. If you bear in mind that about 2,000 instructions are executed for every field in the SELECT list, you

Qualify only the required columns

can recognize the first tuning potential right there, because only in some cases all columns of the row are required. This category also includes the following formulation of an SQL statement:

```
SELECT id
       ,further columns
FROM   table
WHERE  id = :hv-id
```

The field `id` need not be incorporated in the `SELECT` list since it is already uniquely qualified via the host variable. In contrast, the following formulation is correct:

```
SELECT
       id
       ,further columns
FROM
       table
WHERE
       id BETWEEN :hv-id-low AND :hv-id-high
```

Specify all selection conditions

In the SQL statements, the search conditions are not qualified well enough. In that case, after execution of the statement, the unnecessary rows are skipped with an `IF` statement, i.e., by program logic. This type of programming causes superfluous IOs since the Optimizer is not given any chance to fulfill its task, i.e., optimizing the access. A rule of thumb is that the Optimizer should be provided with as much information as possible, so that the number of IOs can be minimized.

Avoid subqueries as far as possible

Subqueries are carried out. The subqueries can be replaced in almost all cases by joins. For joins, the Optimizer generally selects more favorable access paths.

Typical indicators in the Explain for problematical SQL commands are table space scan or index scan, sorting with large result sets, usage of indexes other than those planned, as well as usage of too few index columns.

With repetitive Explains and run tests, the performance of transactions can be restored or, in fact, achieved the first time with this measure. The advantages of this class of tuning measures are the relatively low effort and above all, the local limitation to the processed transaction. There is no fear of negative influences on other transactions with this measure.

Examining the state of the database

If the step described above does not have the desired effects, the next step -- derived from the effort to be employed -- is the examination of the state of the database.

Are the catalog values maintained up-to-date?

For those tables which are required by the transactions coming into consideration, it should be checked whether a RUNSTATS utility has been run before the last bind at all. Cases of these types have definitely happened. The results were dramatic improvements in the response times.

Check the degree of disorganization of the table

Another cause of this problem that is encountered often is the condition of the tables ranging from disorganized to desolate. A frequent cause is that a REORG procedure is never carried out. This successively causes the degradation of the organization degree for all tables -- unless they are pure information tables and are exclusively loaded by a utility. If the CLUSTERRATIO, which can be read from the DB2 catalog drops below 95%, the Optimizer switches to other, less efficient access paths. The following is a sample query for determining the CLUSTERRATIO of indexes that require reorganization:

```
SELECT
        NAME
        , CREATOR
        , TBNAME
        , TBCREATOR
        , COLCOUNT
        , CLUSTERING
        , CLUSTERED
        , CLUSTERRATIO
FROM
        SYSIBM.SYSINDEXES
WHERE
        CLUSTERING = 'Y'
AND     CLUSTERED  = 'N'
```

This class of performance problems can be rectified by regular REORG runs. One important parameter for their frequency is the CLUSTERRATIO mentioned above.

The effect of this method is not as local as the optimization of an SQL statement. Hence, it must always be checked whether any negative influences have been observed for the other accesses to the reorganized table. Cases in which this may happen are, for instance, accesses to tables whose catalog entries have been manipulated manually.

Analyzing the index design

If the examination of the first two classes of problem causes does not yield any solution, the next tuning step is the examination of the index design.

In the previous chapters, it has been shown which main design principles apply for the selection of the indexes. A unique index is required if the uniqueness of the table rows is to be ensured with regard to these fields, i.e., if DB2 should return a return-code on violation of this rule. All further indexes that are not unique are performance indexes. Meaning that they support certain cursor accesses or facilitate economical joins. The clustering index should support the most important or most critical cursor access. The clustering index in particular reduces the IO operations that are actually carried out.

In this step, it is to be checked whether the existing indexes comply with the principles that have just been mentioned or whether a revision of the index design is necessary.

Typical problem causes are an unsuitable clustering index, unused indexes, and, overlapping with the second point, unfavorable index options as, for example, too little PCTFREE in INSERT-intensive tables.

Redesign of indexes has global consequences

Here too, as in the second point, the effects of the measures taken are of a more global nature. This means that it is to be checked, on principle, whether the performance of all the SQL statements accessing the table will still be ensured.

A large part of the performance problems, according to experiences from several tuning projects in which this method was applied, will be solved by taking the measures described so far. These projects confirmed in practice the 80:20 rule mentioned at the beginning. For the next tuning candidates on the hit-list, examination has to be restarted from point 1.

Nevertheless, there will be cases in which you cannot get control by taking the steps described so far. For these transactions, additional tuning steps are described below. Often, these are transactions that have a high CPU time consumption and, at the same time, show conformance between the access profile and Explain.

Examining the program logic

If the examinations carried out so far do not provide any indication of the cause of the problem, or do not achieve the desired effects, the program logic should be examined.

At this point, the tuning measures begin to become costly. If there is a change in the control flow of the program, extensive tests are necessary before the program can be re-launched into production.

In several tuning projects, it turned out that the following two causes occur more often:

* The SQL statements are executed more often than required. This may manifest itself, for example, in too frequent calls of the access modules in which the SQL commands are coded.

* The second cause, which occurs just as frequently, is the execution of single SELECTs instead of a cursor.

Such problem causes cannot be easily recognized from the examinations carried out thus far. An Explain would, for example, grade a single SELECT as optimum. But it does not show that the access occurs in a loop. Some help in analyzing this problem is provided by the access profile that makes transparent the connection between the control flow of the program and the database access.

Changing the business-related requirements on the transaction

If all the examinations carried out so far do not lead to any solution and the response time is still not acceptable, then some thought needs to be given to whether the business-related design represents a dialog at all, or whether an attempt was made to convert a batch process into a transaction.

One approach would be, for example, the implementation of an interactive processing in which the requirements for the batch processing are merely placed in a control table to be carried out later. Another approach would be the initiation of an asynchronous batch processing.

5.4   Expenditure for Tuning

After the repeated execution of such projects, it turned out that tuning can be carried out at a relatively reasonable price by this method.

The tuning of several application systems which required a development effort of about 30 person-years, could be carried out on a budget of about 1.5 person-years. In another example, about 5% of the original development budget was required for the tuning measures. The elapsed time for the first project with a project team of 3 persons on an average was about three-quarters of a year. These team members were not even employed full-time.

5.5   Effort Minimization for Future Tuning Measures

Information about problem causes

The causes of problems have been cataloged and classified in the project report of the first tuning project. These results were incorporated in a check list for the application development and presented to and discussed with the developers in an informational meeting. The other components already discussed above, application scenario and access profile, were further refined in a collaborative effort between some application developers and the database administrators. However, it must be remembered that these aids cannot be used without tool support.

Overall, subsequent tuning activities and projects proved that this method results economically in fast solutions to problems. However, to optimize this procedure the permanent awareness of the developers with regard to the problem causes should be raised.

5.6   Adjustment of the Procedure Model

What has been learned during tuning should be incorporated in activities of the procedure model to minimize the future problem areas. On the one hand, this happens because the DBAs take constructive measures such as check lists and early and extensive support of the projects. On the other hand, this happens through quality assurance measures that are taken immediately before transfer into production, such as program reviews with regard to the SQL statements or Explains.

Both constructive as well as subsequent checking measures must be, as activities, components of the procedure model. Otherwise they are considered either inadequately or not at all in project plans. By timely planning and, of course, by carrying out the QA measures, most of the performance problems mentioned above can be avoided.

5.7   Staff Training

Early involvement
of a DBA

Staff training is a greatly underestimated subject. It became apparent that brief discussions of problem items do not have any lasting effect. With this method, the results that are collected in check lists do not become active knowledge of the developers. A better method, as has already been mentioned above, is the early involvement of DBAs in the projects. With this procedure, a DBA in cooperation with the developer can quickly detect and solve problems in an SQL statement or program. The developer is particularly motivated because it is not some example that is being analyzed, but his program. When intensely analyzing individual SQL statements together with the DBA, the developer will obtain a better understanding of the way the Optimizer works based on influencing factors such as catalog entries. However, this requires a corresponding basic knowledge of the internal processing of the Optimizer. Hence, it is important that clear ideas are given to the developers, e.g., about the different operation methods and the consequences of, for instance, merge scan joins and nested loop joins.

5.8   Measuring the Tuning Results/Success

Some basic conditions have to be taken into consideration when measuring the success of tuning measures.

Probably the best quantifiable measurement criterion is the processor load. In general, the response time correlates with the processor load, but there are additional factors having an effect on the response times that cannot be influenced to a great extent during tuning. Certain batch-runs, e.g., which run in parallel with the on-line operation during the day, can affect the transactions inasmuch as the CPU consumption is not increased, but the elapsed time is.

With the constellation already described at the beginning, namely one transaction code each being assigned for a few programs, the measurability of the tuning effects is facilitated. By comparing the transaction CPU times -- which also include the CPU times in DB2 -- before and after the tuning measures, the success of the activities can be proven with little effort. However, particularly when there are changes to the index design, due attention must be paid to the side-effects on other transactions so that the tuning factor can be determined correctly. In a tuning project with an effort of about 2 person-years, with a 6-processor-machine, one entire processor could be set free mathematically.

So now, where do the problems of the measurement lie or what does "mathematically" imply? When the response time behavior is improved, the end-user can work properly again at last. This means that an increase in the transaction volume is recorded. Hence, in these calculations, care must be taken that the CPU times before and after tuning are comparable. The new CPU times must therefore be standardized according to the old quantity listing. If this step is omitted, the success of the tuning project cannot be proved, and then neither can the economy of the tuning project.

6 Checklists

6.1 Checklist for the Application Development

6.1.1 Tasks of the Application Developers

- Participation in the business-related fine conception of a project
- Creation of the technical conception, supported by DBA group
- Physical application design
  - Data base modeling
  - IO minimization
  - Avoidance of deadlock situations via suitable index design
  - Sparing use of indexes
  - Separate design of batch processing
- Fixed scheduling of reorganization runs (business-related, technical), dynamic execution difficult to plan
- Creation of access profiles
- Programming, test, implementation
- Designation of an application developer as project DBA

6.1.2   Avoidance of Costly Instructions

- Basic objective is IO minimization
- Paying attention to version/release dependencies
- Influencing IO activities by reasonable use of Sequential/List Prefetch
- Operation method of joins
- Implications of SELECT *
- Number of instructions for SELECT
- Table space scan: when is it dangerous or not desirable?

6.1.3   Using Literature

- Administration Guide
- Command and Utility Guide
- Red Books
- See also: Bibliography

6.1.4   Knowledge of Programmers

- Education of software developers, training
- Sensibility of the software developers with regard to IO (IMS programmers)
- Usage of Explain utility

6.1.5   Further Problem Causes

- Locking of resources by debugging tools when setting breakpoints

6.2   Tasks of a DBA Group

6.2.1   Service for Application Development

- Providing tools for the application development relating to DB2, e.g., Explain utility, QA tools

6.2.2   Defining Standards and Conventions

- Authorization standards
- Naming conventions
- Plan standard options
- Use of DDF (Distributed Data Facility)
- Use of RI (Referential Integrity)
- Storage groups vs. user-defined clusters

6.2.3   Monitoring the Production Systems

- Controlling REORG status
- General checking of system load

6.2.4   Quality Assurance

- Acceptance of database design

6.3   Application Scenario

Application Scenario				
Application system			Date	
			Number of calls (target) per	
Procedure	Procedure step	Program	Day	Month
		Total		

6.4   Access Profile

Access Profile									
Program						Date			
	⇐		Target	⇒		⇐		Actual	⇒
SQL statement	Number of calls / proc- essing unit	Tables in target se- quence	Number of pages read	1. x 2. x 0.02		Number of calls / proc- essing unit	Tables in actual se- quence	Number of pages read	3. x 4. x 0.02
	1.		2.			3.		4.	
Elapsed time (approximate value)									

6.5   Checklist for System Design

6.5.1   Application System

- Creating application scenario, i.e., determine and collect the number of targeted calls for each procedure and procedure step in cooperation with the department that will work with the system.

- Regular checking of disk space after implementation in production, at least once a year

6.5.2   Program Design

- Creating an access profile for each main program, considering the program logic

  - Number of calls per processing unit for one SQL

  - Number of pages read per SQL call

  - Number of expected rows per SQL call

- Explain for each access module under production conditions

  - Caution with index scan and table space scan

  - Classifying the SQLs in cost classes (preferably using appropriate DBA tools)

- SQL usage (dependent from release, see Administration Guide)

  - Use only Stage1 and Stage2 predicates, as far as possible

  - Specify only required fields in SELECT clause, avoid SELECT *

  - Use joins instead of subqueries

  - Join with concatenation of multiple join criteria results in table space scan!

  - Index-Only possible?

  - ORDER BY, GROUP BY only with clustering index, as far as possible

  - No DISTINCT, as far as possible, since it implies sorting

- Caution with NOT
- Do not begin LIKE with %
- Use OR with =, otherwise risk of table space scans

6.5.3 Job Design

- Checking whether parallelism is appropriate/necessary/possible
- Using load procedures
- Using Sequential/List Prefetch

6.5.4 Database Design

- Setting up REORG for each large table or tables with frequent modifications
  - technical REORG (utility)
  - business-related REORG (swapping records out)
- Defining clustering index according to the most frequent/critical access, hence no automatic clustering index = unique index
- Sparing use of indexes in dialog systems
  - Small tables: Is index necessary at all?
  - For pure inquiry systems, this point does not apply.
- Aiming for high selectivity of indexes; as far as possible already in the first index column
- Clustering (with appropriate free space parameters) in such a way that deadlocks are avoided; hence no timestamp/date in the first index column of tables with frequent modifications
- Are all the indexes used at all?
- Defining index on join criterion of inner table

6.6   Evaluating the DB2 Catalog for Critical Objects

In the following, some SQL queries are given as examples for searching the DB2 catalog for critical objects. It is advisable to integrate these queries in QMF or other reporting systems since it enables the definition of appropriate forms which improve readability.

6.6.1   Critical Tables

The following queries check possible indicators for critical tables:

- The table has only one column.
- The table has only a few rows.
- No RUNSTATS utility was run for the table.
- The table has no index.
- The table has more than 3 indexes.

```
SELECT
      C.NAME
     ,C.CREATOR
     ,C.DBNAME
     ,C.TSNAME
     ,C.COLCOUNT
     ,C.CARD
     ,C.NPAGES
     ,C.PCTPAGES
     ,C.RECLENGTH - 8
     ,C.ALTEREDTS
     ,C.STATSTIME
     ,COUNT(*)
FROM SYSIBM.SYSTABLES   C
    ,SYSIBM.SYSINDEXES  I
WHERE   C.TYPE      = 'T'
AND     I.TBNAME = C.NAME
AND     I.TBCREATOR = C.CREATOR
AND     (C.COLCOUNT   = 1
    OR   C.CARD       < 10
    OR   C.STATSTIME = '0001-01-01-00.00.00.000000'
        )
GROUP BY
      C.NAME
     ,C.CREATOR
```

```
        ,C.DBNAME
        ,C.TSNAME
        ,C.COLCOUNT
        ,C.CARD
        ,C.NPAGES
        ,C.PCTPAGES
        ,C.RECLENGTH
        ,C.ALTEREDTS
        ,C.STATSTIME
ORDER BY C.CREATOR
         ,C.DBNAME
         ,C.NAME



SELECT
     C.NAME
    ,C.CREATOR
    ,C.DBNAME
    ,C.TSNAME
    ,C.COLCOUNT
    ,C.CARD
    ,C.NPAGES
    ,C.PCTPAGES
    ,C.RECLENGTH - 8
    ,C.ALTEREDTS
    ,C.STATSTIME
FROM SYSIBM.SYSTABLES  C
WHERE  C.TYPE      = 'T'
AND NOT EXISTS (SELECT I.NAME
                FROM   SYSIBM.SYSINDEXES I
                WHERE  I.TBNAME = C.NAME
                AND    I.TBCREATOR = C.CREATOR
               )
ORDER BY C.CREATOR
         ,C.DBNAME
         ,C.NAME
```

```
SELECT
    C.NAME
    ,C.CREATOR
    ,C.DBNAME
    ,C.TSNAME
    ,C.COLCOUNT
    ,C.CARD
    ,C.NPAGES
    ,C.PCTPAGES
    ,C.RECLENGTH - 8
    ,C.ALTEREDTS
    ,C.STATSTIME
    ,COUNT(*)
FROM SYSIBM.SYSTABLES   C
    ,SYSIBM.SYSINDEXES I
WHERE   C.TYPE        = 'T'
AND     I.TBNAME = C.NAME
AND     I.TBCREATOR = C.CREATOR
GROUP BY
    C.NAME
    ,C.CREATOR
    ,C.DBNAME
    ,C.TSNAME
    ,C.COLCOUNT
    ,C.CARD
    ,C.NPAGES
    ,C.PCTPAGES
    ,C.RECLENGTH
    ,C.ALTEREDTS
    ,C.STATSTIME
HAVING COUNT(*) > 3
ORDER BY C.CREATOR
        ,C.DBNAME
        ,C.NAME
```

6.6.2   Critical Table Spaces

Critical table spaces are characterized by the fact that no RUN-STATS was run for them.

```
SELECT  C.NAME
        ,C.CREATOR
        ,C.DBNAME
        ,C.LOCKRULE
        ,C.NTABLES
        ,C.NACTIVE
        ,C.SPACE
        ,C.SEGSIZE
        ,D.PARTITION
        ,D.FREEPAGE
        ,D.PCTFREE
        ,D.PQTY
        ,D.SQTY
        ,C.STATSTIME
FROM SYSIBM.SYSTABLESPACE C
    ,SYSIBM.SYSTABLEPART  D
WHERE C.NAME    = D.TSNAME
  AND C.DBNAME = D.DBNAME
  AND C.STATSTIME = '0001-01-01-00.00.00.000000'
ORDER BY C.CREATOR
        ,C.DBNAME
        ,C.NAME
        ,D.PARTITION
```

6.6.3   Critical Indexes

Indications for critical indexes include:

- Index is defined as clustering index, but it is not clustered.
- Index is not defined as clustering index, but it is clustered.
- Low cardinality of first index column.
- Index level higher than 3.

```
SELECT C.NAME
       ,C.CREATOR
       ,C.TBNAME
       ,C.TBCREATOR
       ,C.UNIQUERULE
       ,C.COLCOUNT
       ,C.CLUSTERING
       ,C.CLUSTERED
       ,C.FIRSTKEYCARD
       ,C.FULLKEYCARD
       ,C.NLEAF
       ,C.NLEVELS
       ,C.CLUSTERRATIO
       ,D.PARTITION
       ,D.PQTY
       ,D.SQTY
       ,D.FREEPAGE
       ,D.PCTFREE

   FROM SYSIBM.SYSINDEXES C, SYSIBM.SYSINDEXPART D
   WHERE C.NAME      = D.IXNAME
     AND C.CREATOR   = D.IXCREATOR
     AND (C.CLUSTERING = 'Y' AND C.CLUSTERED = 'N'
       OR C.CLUSTERING = 'N' AND C.CLUSTERED = 'Y'
       OR C.FIRSTKEYCARD < 10
       OR (C.FULLKEYCARD/C.FIRSTKEYCARD < 5 AND C.COLCOUNT
> 1)
       OR C.NLEVELS > 3
         )

   ORDER BY
         C.TBCREATOR
        ,C.TBNAME
        ,C.CREATOR
        ,C.NAME
        ,D.PARTITION
```

6.6.4   Critical Packages

Critical packages are characterized by the fact that they are

- not valid

or

- not operative.

```
SELECT
     A.NAME
     ,A.OWNER
     ,A.BINDTIME
     ,A.PKSIZE
     ,A.AVGSIZE
     ,A.VALID
     ,A.OPERATIVE
     ,A.PCTIMESTAMP
     ,B.BNAME

FROM SYSIBM.SYSPACKAGE A, SYSIBM.SYSPACKDEP B
WHERE A.LOCATION  = '                     '
   AND A.LOCATION  = B.DLOCATION
   AND A.COLLID    = B.DCOLLID
   AND A.NAME      = B.DNAME
   AND A.CONTOKEN  = B.DCONTOKEN
   AND B.BTYPE     = 'T'
   AND NOT (A.VALID = 'Y' AND A.OPERATIVE = 'Y')

ORDER BY
     A.NAME
     ,A.PCTIMESTAMP DESC
     ,B.BNAME
```

6.7   Inverting a Timestamp

In the following, a sample code for inverting a timestamp is listed in the programming language COBOL. This routine is used to create keys with a uniform distribution.

```
*                   FIELDS FOR CONVERTING
*                   TIMESTAMP
*                   <-> INVERTED TIMESTAMP
*
 05  W-CONV.
    10 W-CONV-TIMESTP          PIC X(26).
    10 FILLER REDEFINES W-CONV-TIMESTP.
       15 W-CONV-TIMESTP-T OCCURS 26
                           PIC X(01).
*
    10 W-CONV-CHAR-20.
       15 W-CONV-CHAR-20-T OCCURS 20
                           PIC X(01).
*
    10 W-CONV-CHAR-1-11.
       15 W-CONV-CHAR-1-10    PIC X(10).
       15 FILLER              PIC 9(01) VALUE 1.
*
    10 W-CONV-PIC9-1-11 REDEFINES W-CONV-CHAR-1-11
                           PIC 9(11).
*
    10 W-CONV-COMP3-CHAR-6.
       15 W-CONV-COMP3-CHAR-5 PIC X(05).
       15 FILLER              PIC X(01) VALUE '1'.
*
    10 W-CONV-COMP3-11 REDEFINES W-CONV-COMP3-CHAR-6
                           PIC S9(11) COMP-3.
*
    10 W-COMV-TIMESTP-IV.
       15 W-CONV-TIMESTP-IV-1-5  PIC X(05).
       15 W-CONV-TIMESTP-IV-6-10 PIC X(05).
* ********************************************************
*                   CONVERTIING TIMESTP TO
*                   TIMESTP-IV
  ********************************************************
      MOVE 20 TO IX-3
*
```

```
       DO CHANGE-1 VARY IX-2 FROM 1 TO 26
          IF IX-2 = 5 OR 8 OR 11 OR 14 OR 17 OR 20
             CONTINUE
          ELSE
             MOVE W-CONV-TIMESTP-T (IX-2)
               TO W-CONV-CHAR-20-T (IX-3)
             COMPUTE IX-3 = IX-3 - 1
          END-IF
       END CHANGE-1
* SINCE PACKED FIELDS IN COBOL MAY NOT HAVE MORE THAN
* 18 DIGITS, PACKING INTO THE TARGET FIELD HAS TO
* BE DONE IN 2 BLOCKS OF 10 DIGITS EACH:
* - TRANSFERRING 10 BYTES IN CHAR-FELD
* - TRANSFERRING 10 DIGITS PLUS APPENDED 1 IN PACKED
*   FIELD WITH 11 POSITIONS
* - TRANSFERRING THE FIRST 5 BYTES OF THE PACKED FIELD
*   ==> THEREFORE, THE BYTE ON THE RIGHT IS OMITTED,
*       I.E., THE APPENDED 1 AND THE SIGN ARE TRUNCATED.
       MOVE W-CONV-CHAR-20 (1:10)
         TO W-CONV-CHAR-1-10
       MOVE W-CONV-PIC9-1-11        TO W-CONV-COMP3-11
       MOVE W-CONV-COMP-3-CHAR-5
         TO W-CONV-TIMESTP-IV-1-5
*
       MOVE W-CONV-CHAR-20 (11:10)
         TO W-CONV-CHAR-1-10
       MOVE W-CONV-PIC9-1-11        TO W-CONV-COMP3-11
       MOVE W-CONV-COMP-3-CHAR-5
         TO W-CONV-TIMESTP-IV-6-10
```

7 Some Additional Stuff for Application Development

7.1 DML Extensions

Some long awaited industry strength extensions concerning DML (data manipulation language) came with DB2 for MVS Version 4 and DB2 for OS/390 Version 5. This section will explain of the following selected extensions:

- AS clause
- CASE expression
- New JOIN types
- SYSDUMMY1 table.

Some other SQL extensions are of comparably minor effect like NULLIF or STRIP or should be considered very carefully like formulating statement specific isolation levels.

7.1.1 AS Clause

Naming of derived columns with the AS clause

Up to now it has always been quite ugly not to be able to name a column in a result set of a query that is derived from an expression or a function. The AS-clause provides a means to name those columns and make the query more readable and handy. So far a simple query with a sum of two columns in the result set had to look like this:

```
SELECT
      col1
      ,col2 + col3
  FROM
      table
  WHERE
      id = :hv-id
  ORDER BY 2 DESC
```

For a specific table the result set might look like this:

```
col1
----  ------
A     9
B     8
C     7
D     6
E     5
F     4
```

Now, with the AS clause, the SELECT-statement can be formulated as follows:

```
SELECT
       col1
      ,col2 + col3 AS sumcol
  FROM
       table
  WHERE
       id = :hv-id
  ORDER BY sumcol DESC
```

The corresponding result set would look again like this:

```
col1   sumcol
----   ------
A      9
B      8
C      7
D      6
E      5
F      4
```

The difference lies not only in improved readability of the result
set alone, but of the query itself. Note that the ORDER BY

clause can make use of the named column.

Another example of the AS clause is using it in the following way:

```
SELECT
        'type1' AS type
        ,col1
        ,col2 * col3 AS arithmetic_col
  FROM
        table1
  WHERE
        id = :hv-id1
UNION ALL
SELECT
        'type2' AS type
        ,col4
        ,col5 + col6 AS arithmetic_col
  FROM
        table2
  WHERE
        id = :hv-id2
  ORDER BY arithmetic_col
```

The query shows that the derived column in the result set can be built differently concerning operators as well as columns. The query recognizes that both columns type and arithmetic_col have the same name in the two result tables and are combined to the following result:

```
type    col1  arithmetic_col
-----   ----  --------------
type1   A     16
type2   B     25
type2   C     36
type1   D     49
type2   E     64
type1   F     81
```

7.1.2   CASE Expression

CASE expression

The next improvement on the usability of queries is the CASE expression. There are three major uses for this expression. First, it can supply the result set with more meaningful contents, secondly, you can handle division by zero, and thirdly, there are possibilities to avoid certain kinds of UNIONs.

Let us come to the more meaningful contents of columns.

```
SELECT
        col1
       ,col2
   FROM
        table
```

This query might have the following result set:

```
col1    col2
-----   ----
A       16
B       25
C       36
D       49
```

Assigning specific values

Using the CASE expression, this query may be rewritten as follows:

```
SELECT
        col1
       ,CASE
          WHEN col1 < 17   THEN 'SMALL'
          WHEN col1 < 43   THEN 'MEDIUM'
          ELSE 'LARGE'
        END
        AS size
   FROM
```

```
table
```

In this case, the query would have the following result:

```
col1    size
-----   ----
A       SMALL
B       MEDIUM
C       MEDIUM
D       LARGE
```

In an application, this usage of the CASE expression might save an extra internal table that maps the values of col2 to the more meaningful values of the size column.

Let's come to the second type of usage, namely to avoid division by zero.

Division by Zero

```
SELECT
      col1
      ,col2 / col3
  FROM
      table
```

This query will end up in problems as soon as there are rows with col3 = 0. Up to now it was impossible to formulate this query in an application. Instead, the division had to take place after testing the division by zero condition in the application program. Now, this problem can be solved much more elegantly, especially without further tests in the application program.

```
SELECT
      col1
      ,CASE
         WHEN col3 = 0   THEN 0
         ELSE col2 / col3
      END
      AS arithmetic_col
  FROM
```

table

You also should notice that the AS-clause is used in the derived column.

Finally, UNIONs can be avoided in certain cases. Again, the AS-clause will be incorporated as well.

Avoiding UNION's

```
SELECT 'type1'
       ,col1
 FROM  table1
 WHERE id < 25

UNION ALL

SELECT 'type2'
       ,col1
 FROM  table1
WHERE id BETWEEN 25 AND 125

UNION ALL

SELECT 'type3'
       ,col1
 FROM  table1
 WHERE id >125
```

Up to now, the subqueries in this full query had to be executed three times to obtain the results. Using a CASE expression the amount of IO and CPU time required could be reduced drastically.

```
SELECT CASE
         WHEN id < 25  then 'type1'
         WHEN id < 126 then 'type2'
         ELSE 'type3'
       END
       AS type
      ,col1
 FROM  table1
```

7.1.3   JOIN Types

As from Version 4 new possibilities to join tables have been made available in DB2. The well known inner join has been supplemented by the new join types left outer join, right outer join and full outer join. How to use these new options will be discussed in the following. The new options will be explained by help of two sample tables table1 and table2.

```
table1                          table2

col1    col2                    col2    col3
-----   ----                    -----   -----
A       23                      110     z3
B       23                      23      z35
C       50                      50      z99
D       70                      70      a351
E       90
```

It is obvious that row (E,90) in table1 and row (110,z3) in table2 do not have a matching row in the other table. With col2 as join column, the formulation and the corresponding results of the different join types will be shown in the following paragraphs.

First, let us deal with the inner join. In addition to it's well known formulation an alternative is supplied.

Inner Join

```
SELECT t1.col1
      ,t1.col2
      ,t2.col3
 FROM  table1 t1
      ,table2 t2
 WHERE t1.col2 = t2.col2
;
```

or

```
SELECT table1.col1
      ,table1.col2
      ,table2.col3
 FROM  table1 INNER JOIN table2
```

```
ON    table1.col2 = table2.col2
;
```

Result of the inner join:

```
col1   col2    col3
-----  -----   -----
A      23      z35
B      23      z35
C      50      z99
D      70      a351
```

Note that, in distinction to the following new join types the un-matched rows in either table will not appear by no means in the result table of the inner join.

left outer join:

Up to now, it was quite elaborate to formulate a left outer join or a right outer join. A left outer join, for example, would require a UNION operator and a correlated subselect:

```
SELECT t1.col1
      ,t1.col2
      ,t2.col3
  FROM  table1 t1
      ,table2 t2
  WHERE t1.col2 = t2.col2

UNION ALL

SELECT '  '
      ,'  '
      ,t2.col3
  FROM table2 t2
  WHERE NOT EXISTS(
      SELECT t1.col1
        FROM  table1 t1
        WHERE t1.col2 = t2.col2
;
```

Alternatively, with the above mentioned tables the left outer join is formulated as follows:

```
SELECT table1.col1
      ,table1.col2
      ,table2.col3
 FROM  table1 LEFT OUTER JOIN table2
 ON    table1.col2 = table2.col2
;
```

This join type will have the following result table:

```
col1   col2   col3
-----  -----  -----
A      23     z35
B      23     z35
C      50     z99
D      70     a351
E      90     (null)
```

At this place, it should be noticed that the unmatched row (E,90) in table1 will appear in the result set. This row is extended by a NULL value in col3.

right outer join:

The formulation of the right outer join is practically the same as the left outer join except using a different keyword:

```
SELECT table1.col1
      ,table1.col2
      ,table2.col3
 FROM  table1 RIGHT OUTER JOIN table2
 ON    table1.col2 = table2.col2
;
```

The result set of the right outer join includes the unmatched row (110,z3) of table2:

```
col1   col2   col3
```

```
-----    -----    -----
A        23       z35
B        23       z35
C        50       z99
D        70       a351
(null)   110      z3
```

Full Outer Join:

Finally, the most complete join type from a result view, the full outer join will be covered. Again, the fomulation of the different join types is alike except using a different keyword:

```
SELECT table1.col1
      ,table1.col2
      ,table2.col3
 FROM   table1 FULL OUTER JOIN table2
 ON     table1.col2 = table2.col2
;
```

The result set of the full outer join includes all unmatched rows from both tables, namely (E,90) from table1 and (110,z3) from table2:

```
FULL OUTER JOIN:

col1     col2     col3
-----    -----    -----
A        23       z35
B        23       z35
C        50       z99
D        70       a351
E        90       (null)
(null)   110      z3
```

With the new join types, it is possible to eliminate some code in application programs that has been necessary so far. In addition to the simplified logic and SQL formulation, IO and CPU time consumption will certainly be improved. Up to now, complicated and time consuming queries for left outer join, right outer join and full outer join have been inevitable.

7.1.4   SYSDUMMY1-Table

Up to now, it has always been necessary to define a system or project specific dummy table to retrieve data not stored in tables, such as special register values or calculations special registers are involved in. In some installations, a whole bunch of these kinds of tables exist and spoil the catalog. DB2 for OS/390 Version 5 provides a new catalog table, namely the SYSDUMMY1 table that can replace all that unpleasant project specific stuff.

```
SELECT
        CURRENT TIMESTAMP
 INTO  :hv-ts
 FROM   SYSIBM.SYSDUMMY1
;
```

In the above example, the value of the current timestamp is placed into the host-variable hv-ts.

7.2   DDL Extensions

In addition to the above mentioned DML extensions that came with DB2 Version 4 and 5, some interesting and very useful new DDL extensions have been supplied as well. The following sections will discuss some selected DDL extensions:

- WITH RESTRICT ON DROP clause

- Type 2 indexes

- Row level locking

- UR – Uncommitted Read

- Stored Procedures

7.2.1   WITH RESTRICT ON DROP clause

WITH RESTRICT ON DROP for safelty reasons

Do you remember the following situation? Just after pressing the Enter key you realized that you made a big mistake: You dropped a table. Did it happen in development or test environment.? So remember, it was only a little bit unpleasant. Some discussions with the project manager. The project that worked on the table was delayed for a few hours and everything was fine again. Or did it happen in production? Uugh, then it was a quite ugly situation, ... all these embarrassing questions from management. And the rollback of the whole financial system to the copy of yesterday evening. Only 200 persons had to do the work of half a day again.

These unpleasant situations can be avoided for the rest of your life. Simply use the following additional clause – always:

```
CREATE TABLE table-name
        .....                        your definitions you always
        .....                        had to supply
        WITH RESTRICT ON DROP
;
```

You will improve your safety by an order of magnitude. Simply dropping the table will not work, you will have to issue the following statement first:

```
DROP RESTRICT ON DROP
;
```

Only after the above statement the DROP TABLE command will work again.

So, why not start improving your safety today?

7.2.2 Type 2 Indexes

With Version 4 a new index type, i.e., the type 2 index has been delivered. Meanwhile a lot of installations have migrated to the new index type. For the others who did not yet, some good reasons will be presented to plan migration to type 2 indexes as soon as possible.

Creating a type 2 index is done within the CREATE INDEX command by the following phrase:

```
CREATE TYPE 2 INDEX index-name
;
```

Enable row level locking

At first, type 2 indexes are the prerequisite to enable row level locking on a table space. Row level locking and its utilization in application development will be treated in a following section.

UR

In the second place, they are mandatory to make use of the new isolation levels uncommitted read and read stability. A discussion of the fields of utilization for uncommitted read follows hereafter.

full partition independence

Next, only with type 2 indexes you can profit from full partition independence. This is particularly relevant for reorganizing partitioned table spaces with non-partitioning indexes. Up to version 3, partition independence was provided only for the clustering index. Locking conflicts for non-partitioning indexes were a hindrance for the REORG utility to run in parallel for several partitions of a particular table space. With type 2 indexes on a partitioned table space it became possible to run the REORG utility for more than one partition at the same time. Consequently, elapsed times for reorganizing partitioned table spaces could be reduced by an order of magnitude.

improved access to DB2 catalog

Finally, some lacking indexes on the DB2 catalog have always been problematic in the respect of locking conflicts on the catalog. This particularly applied to the catalog tables SYSDBRM, SYSFIELDS, SYSFOREIGNKEYS, SYSINDEXPART, SYSKEYS, SYSSTMT, SYSTABLEPART, SYSVIEWS and SYSVOLUMES. Type 2 indexes provide given a tool to reduce locking conflicts on the catalog and improve queries on the catalog. The often implemented solution of building and maintaining a shadow catalog with appropriate indexes to support logical queries on the catalog may see its last days.

Finally let us mention some odd facts that also came with type 2 indexes.

First, we have to live with the fact that type 2 indexes need some more DASD space.

In the second place, if you move to type 2 indexes, you have to do it completely meaning that all indexes on a specific table space have to be of type 2. Mixing of indexes for a specific table space is impossible.

7.2.3   Row Level Locking

As already mentioned, type 2 indexes are a prerequisite for row level locking. Which are the advantages of row level locking from an application development view?

Let us have a look at the DDL first. Row level locking can be defined at tablespace level:

```
CREATE TABLESPACE table-space-name
    IN database-name
    using-block
    free-block
    gbpcache-block
        . . . . .
        . . . . .
    LOCKSIZE ROW
;
```

Better concurrency   In the first place it has to be mentioned that better concurrency is provided. In large production environments with intensively accessed tables there have always been some problems with timeouts or deadlocks. The experience in such environments showed that this problem is at least reduced by far or even eliminated completely at all due to the utilization of row level locking.

Row level locking instead of PCTFREE 99

The standard solution to approach this problem was to set PCTFREE 99 for the above characterized tables. However, it was necessary to have a close look at these critical tables because PCTFREE decreases by changes such as INSERTs. The only way to apply this PCTFREE value again is to reorganize the table rather frequently. Another unpleasant story is the waste of DASD space.

Neglectible locking overhead

With row level locking these complicated and time consuming activities are obsolete. At first glance, there seems to be a slight increase of lock activity by DB2. With LOCKSIZE ANY or LOCKSIZE PAGE one lock per page was requested. The number of locks actually was equal to the number of rows being touched. On the other hand LOCKSIZE ROW practically needs the same number of locks, i.e., the number of rows touched. Consequently, introduction of row level locking for this application scenario does not involve any overhead due to row level locking. It simply provides some advantages concerning maintainability. In other scenarios, however, a slight increase of lock overhead has been noticed.

7.2.4   UR – Uncommitted Read

Some of the most intensively discussed topics during the last years was the DB2 support of uncommitted read, also often called dirty read. Some people hoped to hold the silver bullet in their hands, i.e., to solve every lock problem they had by using this new isolation level. Let us be realistic and have a practical look at it and think about sensible fields of usage.

We start with a brief technical overview. Usage of row level locking can be defined at three different levels: plan level, package level and statement level.

The corresponding syntax reads as follows:

```
BIND PLAN(plan-name)
     OWNER(authorization-id)
     QUALIFIER(aualifier-name)
     MEMBER(xyz)
     ISOLATION(UR)                    <- uncommitted read
     ENABLE(BATCH)
;
```

or

```
BIND PACKAGE(location.collection)
     OWNER(authorization-id)
     QUALIFIER(aualifier-name)
     MEMBER(xyz)
     ISOLATION(UR)                          <- uncommitted read
     ENABLE(BATCH)
;
```

                    or

```
fullselect
     (order-by-clause / update-clause)
     (read-only-clause / optimize clause / with clause)

with -clause:

     with CS
          UR                        <- uncommitted read
          RR
          RS
;
```

Uncommitted read works with type 2 indexes only; so, there is another reason why to move to type 2 indexes.

Now, which application development areas may be relevant for uncommitted read?

CICS applications   First, we will consider an online application like a CICS application. In general, isolation level CS (cursor stability) will be set. Sometimes locking problems will occur, causing timeouts. The intelligent way to solve these problems is to change the involved table spaces to LOCKSIZE ROW. The corresponding command would be:

```
ALTER TABLESPACE tablespace-name LOCKSIZE ROW
;
```

With this measure all correct locking characteristics with respect to concurrency will remain in effect. No changes to the application programs have to be done. Everything will work fine; even the locking problems will disappear. So, why do more? On the contrary, when using uncommitted read, you will have to change the application to ensure the proper concurrency that you had before. Looking for a new thrilling task?

Batch processing

In the second place, we have a look at batch processing. If running exclusively, i.e., not parallel with concurrent other batches or online processing, there always has been a remedy for long elapsed times due to lock overhead:

```
LOCK TABLE table-name IN SHARE MODE
;
```

With this measure, reductions in elapsed time up to 30 percent have been noticed. And it should be considered thoroughly whether it is worthwhile to change a running and stable application for an unknown profit.

Issuing COMMIT

If running in parallel with other applications it has proved to be efficient that the batch program frequently issues commit points. This really is the measure to solve locking problems associated with batch processing.

Warehouse applications

Finally, let us discuss read-only applications like warehouse applications. As there is no update to the tables at all except loading them regularly, there is no need for any locking. So, if you can isolate the warehouse data and the application itself from operational data, you should use a strategy with no locks, i.e., uncommitted read.

Avoid granular isolation levels

To reduce maintenance overhead the isolation level should be defined at a very global level, i.e., plan or package level. It is unlikely to have a good overview and understanding of an application if isolation levels are defined at very granular levels like statements.

Even if there is a chance to isolate tables insofar that they are really read-only you usually cannot isolate the SQL statements upon these tables to the rather global plan or package level. The only way to ensure this is to enforce uncommitted read at statement level. And, as explained before, there are good reasons not to do so.

7.2.5   Stored Procedures

Stored procedures were part of the most awaited extensions of DB2. They have been delivered with Version 4 for the first time, but there have been important limitations that prevented their use, e.g., only scalar values as results. With Version 5, some of these limitations became obsolete. So, which possibilities are there to use stored procedures and, possibly, replace access modules?

It is obvious that reduced network traffic will be obtained with stored procedures as long as there is a sequence of SQL statements that can be executed without interception, e.g., interactions.

At the moment, there are still some restrictions concerning particular SQL statements in a stored procedure. The following SQL statements should not be issued in a stored procedure:

- CALL
- COMMIT
- CONNECT
- RELEASE
- SET CONNECTION
- SET CURRENT SQLID

If one of these statements is activated, it places the DB2 thread in a must rollback state. The calling program can only issue a ROLLBACK statement or terminate itself with an implicit rollback.

Let us consider some arguments concerning the COMMIT statement .

First, in a CICS or IMS environment DB2 cannot commit work. For a detailed discussion of this topic also see the Application Programming and SQL Guide.

Secondly, it is not a clever idea in the sense of application architecture to let someone control work other than the top layer in an application. Otherwise the called programs, e.g., subroutines are not as reusable within the application as they could be.

DB2 for OS/390 Version 5 provides result sets for stored procedures. Handling result sets like retrieved rows of one or more cursors are a prerequisite to supersede access modules. It is possible to pass more than one result set, e.g., result sets with the same or different structures back to the calling application. Handling of result sets will work in the following way. In the stored procedure the cursor associated to the result set must be declared with the return option.

```
DECLARE cursor-name CURSOR WITH RETURN FOR
        select-statement
;
```

When issuing the OPEN CURSOR statement, the cursor will return its complete result set to the calling application. It should be noticed that, in contrast to common application development with access modules the cursor is only opened in the stored procedure; no FETCH or CLOSE statement will be issued herein. With stored procedures FETCH and CLOSE commands are executed in the calling application.

In contrast to access modules specific logic associated with cursors, e.g., stopping the FETCH process within the result set, cannot be written in this direct way. Temporary tables are a workaround for this problem.

What has to be done in the calling application?

First, you have to call the stored procedure and pass parameters to it:

```
CALL stoproc(:paramter1, :parameter2, ...)
;
```

If working with result sets, we have to associate locators after returning from the stored procedure to get the connection to the result sets of the cursors:

```
ASSOCIATE LOCATORS (:l1, :l2, ...) WITH PROCEDURE stoproc
;
```

Next, allocate the cursor for the result set

```
ALLOCATE c1 CURSOR FOR RESULT SET :l1
;
```

and fetch the cursor in the well-known manner until an end

condition.

```
FETCH c1 USING ...
;
```

Up to now, i.e., Version 5, there is no way to call the stored procedure with a structure commonly used in COBOL programs. Instead you have to pass variable by variable to the stored procedure. This is a disadvantage compared to access modules used so far.

As already mentioned, only complete result sets of cursors can be passed to the calling application. Processing non relational data or specific logic like cursors with only some fetches or cursors opened, fetched, closed and then reopened have to be placed into a temporary table that can be passed to the calling application. Usually this will be done like that:

```
CREATE GLOBAL TEMPORARY TABLE temp-table-name
       LIKE original-table-name, ...)
;
```

The original table name is the name of the table the cursor is acting on. Every relevant fetched row has to be inserted into the temporary table. Again, another cursor has to be declared for return and opened upon this temporary table. The contents of the temporary table will be made available to the calling application.

At first glance this looks a little bit awkward, but maybe we are simply not used to this kind of programming.

As a conclusion there are still some reasons to use access modules in a CICS environment, especially because of structures that can be passed to stored procedures and the flexibility with returning result sets to the calling application. Nevertheless, for a lot of cases stored procedures can be used right now.

Bibliography

[1]   Denne, Norbert: DB2 Theorie und Praxis, DGD-Verlag,
      1992, ISBN 3-929187-00-0

[2]   IBM DB2 V4 Administration Guide, SC26-3265-00

[3]   IBM DB2 V4 Utility Guide and Reference, SC26-3395-00

[4]   IBM DB2 V3 Performance Topics, GG24-4284-00

[5]   IBM DB2 V5 Administration Guide, SC26-8957-00

[6]   IBM DB2 V5 Application Programming and SQL Guide,
      SC26-8958-00

[7]   IBM DB2 V5 Utility Guide and Reference, SC26-8967-00

[8]   IBM DB2 V2.2 Design Guidelines for High Performance,
      GG24-3383-00

[9]   IBM DFSORT Application Programming: Guide Release
      11,
      SC33-4035-14

[10] Hoover, Chuck: Understanding the DB2 Version 3 Buffer
      Manager, Compuware Chuck Hoover Series, 1995

[11] Mullins,Craig S.: DB2 Developer's Guide, 1994,
      ISBN 0-672-30512-7

Index

—A—

access path 18, 54
access profile 32, 33, 102, 103, 106,
  107, 108, 111, 117
ALTER 8, 63
application scenario 31, 32
arithmetic in SQL statement 53

—B—

batch run 34
batch runtime 5
blocking factor 40
breakpoint 112
buffer pool 34, 36, 82, 87
bulk deletions 7
business object 83, 84, 87, 89, 90
business transaction 32
business-related unit of work 66
BuTra-Assign table 66
BuTra-Control table 66

—C—

cache 82, 87
checkpoint frequency 7
CLUSTER 86, 87, 90, 91
clustering 8, 16, 18, 23, 25, 28, 29
CLUSTERRATIO 43, 93, 105
COMMAREA 48
COMMIT 59, 60
Commit route 6, 28
concatenation 79
cost factor 55

CREATE 53
CREATOR 53

—D—

DCL 53
DDL 53
deadlock 7, 14, 92, 95, 111
debugging tool 112
DEFER 27
DELETE CASCADE 55
delete flag 41
denormalization 72
disposition table 9
distributing 11, 12, 15, 28
distribution of attributes 73, 74, 78
dynamic quality 52
dynamic SQL 77

—E—

encapsulation 45, 48, 49
EQUALS 42
error handling 50
expanding tables 52
Explain 103, 104, 106, 107, 112, 113,
  117
EXPLAIN 54, 80, 81

—F—

filtering 38
fine conception 111
FULLKEYCARD 22, 26

—G—

generic key 46
GETPAGE 86, 88, 89, 91
GRANT 53

—H—

hiper pool 82, 87
host variable 54
hot-spots 10, 11, 15, 28, 57, 84, 91
Hot-spots 28
Hot-Spots 85

—I—

IAA 83
indexable 55
INDEXLEVEL 11, 21, 29
initial contents 12
INSERT 54
inversion 11, 12, 69
IO minimization 111, 112

—J—

join 54

—L—

LOAD 8, 9, 25, 27
load file 41, 42
load procedure 9, 28, 29, 39, 40, 92, 94,
    96, 97, 118
Load Replace 39, 41, 42, 43
Load Resume 39, 43
lock table 58, 62, 63, 64, 65
lock type 58, 59, 61, 62, 63, 64, 65
locking 5, 6, 7, 8, 9, 10, 14, 15, 28, 68,
    95, 112
Locking 28
log data set 92, 94

LOG NO 93, 97, 98

—M—

macro 49
MATCHCOLS 75, 81
Matching Index Scan 81
multi-path Join 19

—N—

naming conventions 50
nested-loop join 75

—O—

OMIT 97
OPTIMIZE 23, 28, 93

—P—

package 103
page-split 12
parallel 94, 96, 97
parallelism 45, 118
partition 8, 25, 40, 41, 95, 98
Partition 98
PCTFREE 8, 12, 28, 63, 64, 65, 106
permitted commands 50
PLAN_TABLE 55
prefetch 35, 36, 37
Prefetch 24, 112, 118
preload 12, 19, 63, 65
Preload 28
preprocessor run 49
procedure 32
procedure model 31, 32
processing logic 24, 29
programmed join 17

—Q—

quality assurance 52
quantities 32
query block 76, 77
query manipulation 18
queue 57, 58, 60, 92
queuing 5, 14, 15
Queuing 28

—R—

REBIND 95, 97
RECOVER 95, 96
reducing indices 9
referential integrity 17, 53, 55
relation entities 83, 85, 86, 87, 88
release change 100
REORG 8, 9, 12, 25, 27, 28, 63, 93, 105,
    111, 118
REPLACE 40, 41, 42, 43
response time 33
restart clause 79
restart condition 39, 80
restart keys 57
restart logic 6
restart procedures 50
RESUME 25
re-use 47
REVOKE 53
RUNSTATS 18, 20, 28, 105

—S—

search conditions 104
SELECT * 52
selectivity 21, 22, 26, 28, 29, 118

sequential prefetch 93
sorting 75
special character 69
Stage1 55
Stage2 55
standard access 45, 46
static quality 52
status flag 60, 61, 62, 63, 64
subquery 20, 117
synchronous IO 9, 16, 23, 29, 82, 88
SYNCPOINT 59, 66, 77

—T—

table columns 54
table number 68, 71
technical conception 111
time-out 59, 60, 61, 62, 64
tuning 100, 101, 102, 103, 104, 106, 107,
    108, 109, 110
Tuning 101, 108, 110

—U—

user behavior 100

—V—

validity flag 7

—W—

WHENEVER 53
WHERE clause 17
WITH DEFAULT 8
WITH HOLD 39, 77
WRITE 40, 43

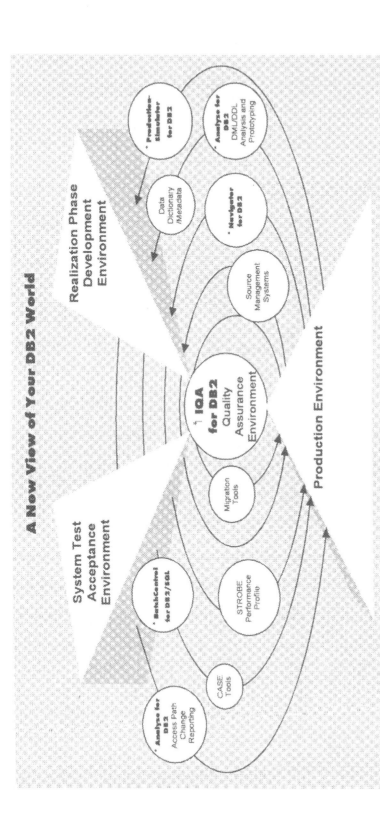

With □ *IQA for DB2, all development tools are integrated by a comprehensive user interface. This integration includes software products from 3rd party venders. Thus, providing a look and feel of a single quality assurance tool.*

SOFTWARE ENGINEERING GmbH
Robert-Stolz-Strasse 5
D-40470 Düsseldorf
Germany
Tel.: +49/211/96149-0
Fax.:+49/211/96149-32

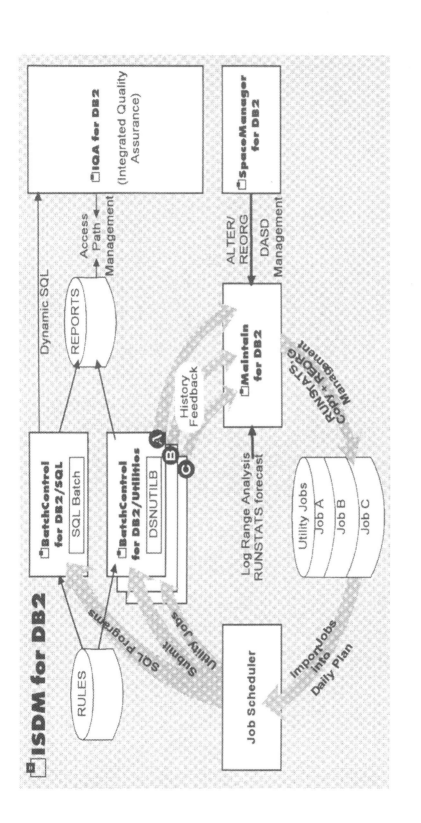

Svein-Olaf Hvasshovd

**Recovery in Parallel
Database Systems**

2. Ed. 1999. xx, 302 pp. with 71 figs.
Softc. DM 118,00
ISBN 3-528-15411-X

Contents: Basic Concepts - DBMS
Recovery Requirements - Analysis
of Centralised DBMS Transaction
and Node Crash Recovery
Approaches - The Block Oriented
Approach - The Record Oriented
Approach - The Compensation
Oriented Approach - The Table
Oriented Approach - The Hyper Re-
lational Approach - The Location
and Replication Independent Tuple
Recovery Strategy - The Log Distri-
bution Strategy - The Neighbour Write-
Ahead Logging Strategy - Maintaining
a Continuously Available Transaction
Server

This book presents and analysis in a
systematic way the main recovery
approaches for centralised DBMSs
developed over the last two decades,
in particular to how well they fulfil
the requirements for availability and
soft real-time response. The analysis
relates specifically to approaches
used in current commercial and
research systems. The element in
particular lacking in the current
methods is the ability to on-line re-
establish the faulttolerance level
automatically and without blocking.
A set of novel recovery methods for
parallel DBM's based on multi-
computer shared nothing hardware
is presented. The recovery methods
are intended to support: Continuously available transaction services,
very high transaction loads, and soft
real-time transaction response.

vieweg

Abraham-Lincoln-Straße 46
D-65189 Wiesbaden
Fax 0611. 78 78-400
www.vieweg.de

Stand 1.10.99. Änderungen vorbehalten.
Erhältlich im Buchhandel oder beim Verlag.

Bernd-Ulrich Kaiser

**Corporate
Information
with SAP®-EIS**
Building a Data
Warehouse and a MIS-
Application with inSight

1998. xii, 206 pp. with 44 figs.
Hardc. DM 198,00
ISBN 3-528-05674-6

Contents: Information needs and
information sources - Data ware-
housing - inSight® for SAP®-EIS
from arcplan - Building and maintaining an Management Information System (MIS)

The book is a real life-oriented, professional guide to developing a Management Information System (MIS).
The book is professional in the sense
that it adresses an MIS that encom-
passes all the hierarchical decisions-
making levels within a corporation,
and it emphasizes reliable, under-
standable and transparent information. The most important demand of
an MIS is an easy-to-use-system
interface, which needs to be coupled
with an information infrastructure
that takes marked conditions and
the company´s particular business
invironment into account. The use of
a modular and flexible system architecture is designed to maximize the
system´s benefits to cost ratio. In
addition to SAP-EIS, the book details
how to use the inSight program
(from the Duesseldorf-based company arcplan) to optimize system
perfomance.

vieweg

Abraham-Lincoln-Straße 46
D-65189 Wiesbaden
Fax 0611. 78 78-400
www.vieweg.de

Stand 1.10.99. Änderungen vorbehalten.
Erhältlich im Buchhandel oder beim Verlag.

Printed in the United States
By Bookmasters